To Dean Ray
Judith Herb College of Education
Enjoy the story of a
Toledo product development
that has now touched
practically everyone on
this planet!

Tom Brady

History of the PET Bottle

from an O-I/PTI Perspective

By Dr. Tom Brady

VP, Plastics Technology at Owens-Illinois (O-I) 1972-1985

Founder, Plastic Technologies, Inc. (PTI) 1985-2022

This publication contains the ideas and opinions of its author. It is intended to provide helpful and informative material on the topics addressed in the publication and it is based on the author's knowledge and recollection of events, related to the best of his knowledge. Incidents are related to highlight issues and are not intended to portray any given company or individual in a negative light. The author does not assume and hereby disclaims any liability to any party for any loss, damage, or disruption caused by errors or omissions, whether such errors or omissions result from accident, negligence, or any other cause.

Direct any comments or questions or requests for an electronic copy of this book to: drtombrady1944@gmail.com
Bound copies of this book can be purchased from Amazon or from any bookstore

Acknowledgements

A history, by definition, is a collection of memories, analyzed and reduced to meaningful conclusions. However, this history of the PET Bottle is as much a collection of the memories of those industry and PTI colleagues who created that history as it is of my own memories.

Industry and PTI colleagues who contributed memories and photographs and who have helped me write and edit this story include, in alphabetical order: Jack Ardrey, John Bachey, Forrest Bayer, Martin Beck, Brittanie Begamen, Betsy Brady, Long Fei Chang, Bob Deardurff, Jeff DeGross, John Dunagan, Dan Durham, Thierry Fabozzi, Saleh Jabarin, Chuck Kern, Gunter Kleimenhagen, Jean-Pierre Lanctuit, Randy Litten, John Maddox, Sumit Mukherjee, Mark Niemiec, Missy Otterson, George Rollend, Peter Rose, Dick Roswech, Paul Rothschild, Robert Schad, Frank Schloss, Scott Steele, and Dan Weismann.

I have also relied upon US patents, documentaries, and news articles published by important industry trade journals and universities including, Plastics News Magazine, Plastics World Magazine, Industry Week Magazine, The Glass Factory Yearbook and Directory, The Gloucester Times, and the University of Toledo Archives, and I want to recognize and thank Mr. Tom Ethington who for most of PTI's history was our official company photographer, since many of the photos in this book came from Tom's archives.

John Dunagan deserves a special thanks because it was John who conceived of the Coca-Cola Cooperative coalition in 1985 and it was John who approached me to ask whether I would leave my secure job at O-I and help the Coca-Cola Cooperatives build a self-manufacture capability. So, I owe John Dunagan a huge thank you for convincing me to leave O-I and to embark on what has been an unbelievably exciting and rewarding 36-year career as the PTI Founder and now Chairman Emeritus.

Most importantly, I owe this entire history, as well as this summary of that history, to my wife and best friend, Betsy Brady, who not only enthusiastically encouraged and supported me in this endeavor for the past 36 years but who also created and managed the administrative, financial, personnel, and cultural aspects of all the PTI companies from the very beginning.

And as will be clear through the course of this book, so many others have been integral to this amazing journey, including company leaders, employees, customers, vendors, innovators, supporters, advisors, and partners of all stripes. All their contributions and heartbeats live on through the memories and stories and pictures here, and the PTI of the future which is still being shaped. My deepest appreciation to all who have been a part of it!

Table of Contents

Page

4	O-I from 1972 to 1985
6	First Plastic Soft Drink Bottle
7	O-I's Soft Drink Bottle Development Effort
9	O-I's Oriented Polymer Focused Effort
12	The Acrylonitrile Story
15	More About the Early Competition Between ANS and PET
17	The PET Decision
21	The Goodyear PET Resin Industry Story
24	The Evolution of Goodyear's PET Business
24	Shell Acquires Goodyear's Polyester Business
24	M&G Acquires Shell's Polyester Business
25	The Eastman Chemical Company Story
27	Plastics News Magazine – Dave Cornell
31	O-I's Plastic Beverage Operations
37	Plastic Beverage Operations Technical Center
43	O-I's Milford CT Plant
45	Beyond Milford CT
46	The End of PET at O-I
49	Industry Situation and Early PTI History
50	Evolution of the PET Bottle Industry
53	Early History of the PET Bottle Industry
55	Importance of the Coca-Cola Company
56	The Petainer PET Plastic Can Story
62	Coca-Cola's Influence on the PET Recycling Industry
64	The Development of the PepsiCo PET Returnable Bottle
67	The Story of Husky Injection Molding Systems
70	History of the Sidel Group SL
78	The Story of Plastic Technologies, Inc.
83	PTI Today
100	The PTI Family of Companies
101	Phoenix Technologies International LLC
104	PTI Europe SARL
106	The Packaging Conference
107	PTI Operations (Preform Technologies LLC)
111	Guardian Medical USA
114	PTI New Business Development
116	Industry Publications Documenting PTI's Story
126	Tom's Plastic Packaging Industry Museum
131	The Future – The Case for a Circular Economy

O-I from 1972 - 1985

"I want to say just one word to you, son .... Plastics!"
From the 1967 motion picture, The Graduate, starring Dustin Hoffman

Having just watched the movie "The Graduate" and then graduating myself from the University of Michigan in 1972 with a PhD in Plastic Materials Engineering, I was hired as a **Senior Plastics Technology Associate** by **Owens-Illinois. Inc. (O-I)**.

I vividly recall my first day at the O-I Technical Center which, as it happened, was a premonition of (what became) the future.

My boss, Dr. Gerry Miller, started me out with a tour of the Technical Center which, at the time, was where O-I carried out all the R&D for glass, metal, paper, and plastics packaging.

O-I North Technical Center 1972

Today, O-I has retrenched to become a glass container business only, but back then O-I was a full-service packaging company with a Plastic Products Division that was one of the leading plastic container producers in the country, with 18 plants nationwide that made polyethylene (PE), polyvinyl chloride (PVC), and polystyrene (PS) containers, closures, labels, and multipack carriers.

As we toured the Glass Container research laboratories, I still remember looking through the window into one of the labs where a man standing on a 12-foot ladder and wearing what looked like a protective white spaceman's suite was dropping 64 oz. glass bottles filled with carbonated liquids to test their resistance to shattering when dropped.

Drop Testing a 32 oz (coated) Glass Bottle

I also noted that every bottle shattered and that the man on the ladder always looked away and covered his face with his hands. I later learned that the protective suit was indeed to shield the technician from exploding glass shards and that the bottles were coated with **Surlyn™** plastic (the same plastic used to coat golf balls), with the objective of discovering a way to make large glass bottles filled with carbonated liquids safe. Soon after my tour and almost before I was even assigned a desk, I learned from Dr. Miller that Coca-Cola had recently asked O-I and its other packaging suppliers to create options for "family-sized" beverage containers so they could sell more product.

12 oz Glass Bottles - 1972

Back then, you may recall that the only glass and metal container options were 12 oz or smaller because, as it turns out, it is nearly impossible to make large sized metal and glass containers that are both safe and economical. My tour of the O-I Technical Center that first day was indeed a premonition of my now 50-year career in the plastic packaging industry because it was obvious to Dr. Miller and to the other plastics executives at O-I, and even to me after that first tour, that the only way to make family-sized carbonated soft drink containers was going to be to figure out a solution with plastics!

Of course, plastics had never been used for carbonated soft drinks up until that time because the then-common commodity plastics such as polyethylene (PE), polyvinyl chloride (PVC), and polystyrene (PS) were very permeable to O_2 and CO_2, so they could not offer sufficient shelf life for commodity soft drink packaging. Nor could commodity plastics offer enough strength to resist expansion when exposed to the internal pressures of 60-100 psi as in carbonated soft drinks.

2L PET Bottle with a PE Base Cup

Some of the engineering plastics like nylon and polycarbonate (PC) did offer somewhat better permeability resistance (nylon) or strength and drop impact resistance (PC), but they also had their limitations, including having property limitations such as opacity (nylon), or strength and cost (PC).

Other package and material suppliers were, of course, getting the same message from Coca-Cola and from PepsiCo and from all the carbonated soft drink manufacturers, so the race to offer a commercial option began just as I walked into my first job at O-I.

As it turns out, I hit the jackpot and was offered the "opportunity of a lifetime." After all, how many people get the chance to help start an entire and lasting industry? Well, let's say that I and my colleagues at O-I got that chance back in the early 1970's and, I am happy to say, we seized the opportunity and "made it happen."

First Plastic Soft Drink Bottle

To be clear, we were not the only ones pursuing the dream although my story will, of course, focus on the O-I and subsequently the PTI stories. Several other companies put together efforts like ours at O-I, with the goal of developing a commercial plastic bottle option for the carbonated soft drink brand owners.

Monsanto acrylonitrile Lopac ™ Bottles

Continental Can and Amoco (which became Silgan) were all early competitors to O-I. Soon after that, companies like Sewell Plastics (which became Constar), Hoover Universal (which became Amcor), Graham Packaging, International Beverage, and PlastiPak all jumped into the PET beverage bottle competition.

However, it was Monsanto that commercialized the very first **EASY GOER™** plastic carbonated soft drink bottle in 1973 using their trademarked acrylonitrile (AN) resin, **Lopac™**, which also had the required permeability and strength properties for carbonated beverages.

Three Monsanto plants came online in 1975 to produce the 32 oz **Lopac™** bottles, but in 1975 and soon after that bottle hit the market, the FDA declared AN to be carcinogenic, which eliminated AN as a commercial option. That FDA ruling took Monsanto and Sohio's Vistron Division, which was also developing an acrylonitrile option trade named **Barex™**, out of the market.

O-I's Soft Drink Bottle Development Effort

Interestingly, the AN approach was also being hotly pursued by O-I and, in fact, in the laboratory right next to our Polymer Materials and Processes Laboratory at the O-I Technical Center in Toledo was a chemistry lab where O-I chemists, Bill Bayer, Jim Crawford, Dr. Bob Fechter, and Tom Marino all worked feverishly for several years to develop an acrylonitrile-styrene copolymer which would compete with Monsanto's **Lopac™**, but which would be proprietary to O-I.

Paul Rothschild

In addition to O-I's internal acrylonitrile polymer development effort, and to assure O-I of having a competitive option, Paul Rothschild, Plastics R&D Director, and Dr. Gerry Miller, Manager of the Plastics Materials and Processing Laboratory, jointly led a parallel effort to develop a relationship with the DuPont Company for the purpose of leveraging DuPont's polymer chemistry expertise to develop an AN polymer option which O-I could commercialize to compete with Monsanto.

However, when the FDA decision on AN was published in 1975, O-I immediately abandoned all the AN copolymer development work and those same chemists began working to understand other homopolymer and copolymer compositions, since the goal of developing a plastic soft drink bottle was still alive and well.

Dr. Saleh Jabarin

The Polymer Materials and Processing Laboratory that I worked in did all the evaluations of the experimental AN resins that were produced in the O-I Polymer Chemistry Laboratory and, interestingly, among the other scientists and engineers in our laboratory was a former Dartmouth College classmate of mine, Dr. Saleh Jabarin.

After graduating from Dartmouth as a chemistry major in 1966, Saleh earned his master's degree in Polymer Chemistry from Brooklyn Polytechnic Institute and his PhD in Polymers at the University of Massachusetts under the tutelage of the famous Polymer Engineering Professor, Dr. Richard Stein.

I also received my Bachelor of Arts degree with a major in Engineering Science from Dartmouth in 1966, but I stayed at Dartmouth for my master's degree in Engineering Science and then moved on to the University of Michigan where I earned a PhD in Plastic Materials Engineering in 1972, under the tutelage of Dr. Gregory Yeh.

7

Saleh and I did not know each other at Dartmouth since I was in Engineering and he was in Chemistry, but as it happens, we ended up almost back-to-back in adjacent offices within a matter of several months, after we were both hired to work in the O-I Polymer Materials and Processing Laboratory in 1972, then under the direction of Dr. Gerald W. Miller.

As two newly hatched PhD's, Saleh and I obviously did not have much industrial experience, but our degrees and our respective graduate studies were both ideally suited for the challenge that O-I was undertaking, so we were almost immediately assigned major responsibility for the development of the fundamental technologies that would be required to design and manufacture a commercial carbonated soft drink container.

Again, we were both a bit lucky since we just happened to be "in the right place at the right time!"

Saleh was assigned responsibility for developing a fundamental understanding of polymer materials technologies related to making a commercial soft drink container, and I was assigned responsibility for developing a fundamental understanding of the polymer processing technologies that would be required.

Prototypes of and O-I's first commercial 32 oz PepsiCo PET Bottle

Beginning in 1971 with no obvious commercial materials and processing options and culminating in 1976 with the commercial production of O-I's first commercial PepsiCo 32 oz bottle in Milford CT, that five years was indeed a wild, exciting, and fun ride, and not just for Saleh and me but for the entire O-I technology development and manufacturing team, and I am sure the ride was equally wild and exciting for each of O-I's competitors.

O-I's Oriented Polymers Focused Effort

Chuck Plymale

O-I's plastics technology management team, including Chuck Plymale, Dr. Gerry Miller, Paul Rothschild, and Jim Heider, recognized early on that in order to make a functional soft drink container with sufficient drop impact resistance, sufficient strength, and low enough permeability at a reasonable weight, any plastic used in that application would have to exhibit enhanced properties; simply blow molding a container shape using standard methods was probably not going to create a container with enhanced physical, chemical, and transport (permeability) properties.

While I don't know exactly who in the O-I hierarchy organized the plan and pulled the trigger, almost immediately after Saleh and I arrived at O-I a formal and comprehensive R&D program was announced and named the **"Oriented Polymer Focused Effort"** to develop a comprehensive understanding of how two-dimensional molecular orientation could enhance the properties of any commodity polymer that might be used for any plastic container, but more specifically to understand how orientation would enhance the properties of plastics used for carbonated soft drink containers.

James Heider

For clarity, plastics are made of very long chain molecules and those long chains can be stretched out and frozen in place, if a plastic is stretched at temperatures just below the melting point but above the softening point.

This molecular alignment can happen in either one dimension (uniaxial extension, as happens in the drawing of textile fibers) or in two dimensions (biaxial extension, as in the manufacture of polyester **Mylar™** sheet or film).

When the PET molecules become aligned in either one or two-dimensional stretching, and if that "orientation" is frozen in place, the plastic film or sheet or fiber or blown bottle becomes significantly stronger, more drop resistant, and less permeable to gases.

In the case of PET, that molecular alignment also causes the molecules to "fit together," which is what we call "crystallization." Aligned molecules that are crystallized are 10x stronger and 10x less permeable than unoriented and uncrystallized molecules, which is why oriented PET bottles are so well suited for carbonated soft drinks and for other plastic bottle packaging product applications.

Also, because PET polyester (the technical name is polyethylene terephthalate) is manufactured in high volumes, it is considered a "commodity" plastic which makes it a relatively low-cost plastic, so PET is commonly used for everything from polyester fibers and films to PET bottles.

Again, being in the right place at the right time, Saleh and I were assigned leadership roles in creating and conducting that oriented polymer focused effort which, as it turns out, was crucial for the eventual development of a commercial plastic bottle that could compete with glass and metal.

A Biaxial Extensometer for Plastic Sheet

O-I acquired what was then known as a "Long Biaxial Sheet Extensometer" a long name for a device that would allow the deformation (stretching) of square sheets in two dimensions at variable stretching rates, to variable x-y dimensions, and at variable temperatures, so that we could study the effects of biaxial orientation on the properties of any plastic.

In collaboration with the O-I Plastics Processing Laboratory personnel, including Jim Heider, Greg Fehn, Nick Curto, John Kidwell, and Dick Morrette, we began by stretching and studying the effects of biaxial orientation on the properties of polyvinyl chloride (PVC), but we also studied the biaxial orientation of polycarbonate (PC), acrylonitrile (AN), polypropylene (PP), polyethylene (PE) and eventually, of PET (polyester), which became the material of choice for creating an economically feasible plastic soft drink container.

Dr. Long Fei Chang

Saleh and I managed the entire orientation program from a materials perspective. With the assistance of Dr. Long Fei Chang, another (then) O-I Senior Scientist with a mathematical background who worked in the Computer Science Laboratory, we eventually developed algorithms and correlations so that we could predict the properties and the performance of containers made from virtually any material formed under almost any set of processing conditions.

I still believe that our work in this field was what put O-I in a leadership position when it came to designing optimum preforms for the successful high speed commercial production of plastic soft drink containers; and I still have the 3-inch-thick reports that we wrote to summarize our findings during this 3-year race to the commercial production of oriented PET containers.

Dr. Long Fei Chang eventually moved from O-I to the University of Toledo's Polymer Institute to work for Dr. Jabarin, who himself had left O-I several years earlier to create the UT Polymer Institute (that's another interesting story). Dr. Chang then came to my company, Plastic Technologies, Inc. (a story which I will relate later) in 1987. He was then and still is, at an advanced age, the technical expert who developed the early proprietary PET preform design programs and technology that gave O-I an early advantage in the emerging plastic beverage bottle industry. And interestingly, Dr. Chang still uses the data in those 3-inch-thick reports that I wrote many years ago!

During those first several years Dr. Chang, Dr. Saleh Jabarin, Paul Rothschild, Jim McCornock, Bob Fey, Andy Dickson, and I travelled together to Japan and Europe and Canada to study what Toyo Seiken and others were learning about orientation, and we even purchased newly designed polypropylene (PP) orientation blow molding equipment machinery from Mitsui Toatsu and installed it in our Florence, KY plant to make the first oriented and clear PP bottles for P&G's Dawn detergents.

To be fair, I don't have the details of what our worthy competitors, primarily Continental Can/Continental PET Technologies, were doing during those early years. But judging from (now) a view of history and after watching PTI remain one of the leaders in the PET package development arena, using essentially the same people we trained and the technologies that we developed at O-I, I think it is fair to conclude that indeed O-I did develop the most comprehensive understanding in the industry of how orientation affects properties, from a fundamental polymer chemistry viewpoint.

In fact, PTI technologists today, under the direction of Mr. Sumit Mukherjee, PTI Chief Technical Officer, have developed and routinely use even more sophisticated digital computer simulation technology which we call **Virtual Prototyping™** which allows PTI to design, manufacture, test, and predict the properties of any plastic container of any shape and size, all on the computer, and without ever even fabricating an experimental prototype.

To be clear, we do still manufacture millions of prototype containers at PTI. But today we have such a comprehensive mathematical understanding of PET manufacturing and orientation processes that we can literally design, manufacture, and test a PET container "virtually" in a matter of hours.

The Acrylonitrile (AN) Story

Even though this is the story of the PET bottle that eventually became the winner in the race to find a commercial plastic option, it is worth digressing for just a bit to tell the story of AN, specifically the copolymer polyacrylonitrile-styrene, because AN really did win the early race and except for an ill-fated decision by the FDA and perhaps another ill-fated decision by Coca-Cola's marketing department, AN could perhaps still be the choice for today's barrier packaging where resistance to the permeation of oxygen and carbon dioxide is required.

Even telling the story of AN requires acknowledging that the eventual winner of the AN race, Monsanto, had competition as far back as the early 1960's.

In fact, during the early 1960's Sohio's Vistron Division also developed an acrylonitrile-styrene copolymer option and named it **Barex™** (stands for Barrier Acrylonitrile Resin, Extrusion Grade) which was commercially available even before Monsanto's AN resin, **Lopac™** (stands for Low Oxygen Permeability Packaging).

However, Monsanto was apparently better focused on the commercial prize and hired McKinsey & Co. in the 1960s to study how it could coordinate its resources better. McKinsey found that several other companies were also working on developing low permeability plastics, so they advised Monsanto to develop a plastic bottle specifically for either beer or soft drinks.

Michael Gigliotti

In 1968, Monsanto executives assigned Michael Gigliotti to lead the **Lopac™** development project. Gigliotti quickly contacted Allen Heininger who was head of Monsanto's food flavoring and ingredients business, and they both went to their bottle manufacturing experts at Plax Corporation which Monsanto had purchased 10 years earlier, to see if Plax could make sample bottles quickly.

Heininger then took Gigliotti on a whirlwind tour to meet the top beer executives Augie Busch and Jeffrey Coors, and to meet J Paul Austin, Coca-Cola Company President, and Robert Woodruff, former Coca-Cola Company President and then Chairman of the Coca-Cola Company Board of Directors. Robert Woodruff was still acknowledged to be the most influential person in the Coca-Cola Company, and he was still behind all key decisions made by the company, including the selection of Roberto Goizueta as the new Chairman and CEO of Coca-Cola in 1981. Many people referred to Mr. Woodruff back then simply as "The Boss" or "Mr. Anonymous"

Gigliotti's proposal to each CEO and to Mr. Woodruff was that Monsanto would send them small bottles to test, but that they would not identify the material. Monsanto then quickly manufactured, tested, and sent out bottle samples made from several resins, including PET, polystyrene, and ethylene vinyl alcohol, but the unidentified material was acrylonitrile-styrene copolymer. The in-house testing as well as the results from the brand owners told Monsanto very quickly that PET and acrylonitrile offered the best combination of properties and cost.

Concerned that Coca-Cola might lose significant market share or that PepsiCo would beat Coca-Cola to the plastic bottle market, Coca-Cola's product manager pushed commercialization, even though others at Coca-Cola were concerned that plastic would impact the taste.

My understanding is that Robert Woodruff convinced Coca-Cola's CEO to take the gamble and Coca-Cola announced in 1973 that Coca-Cola was ready to buy Monsanto's entire plastic bottle capacity, and Coca-Cola backed that up, the story goes, by sending Monsanto a check for $1 million!

After caucusing for just a few minutes, the Monsanto officials reportedly proposed giving Coca-Cola rights to 85 percent of Monsanto's nameplate bottle capacity in exchange for Coca-Cola's financing of the required future research and experimental work. Coca-Cola then rolled out a big consumer research program which included the distribution of plastic AN bottles filled with Coca-Cola. When consumers snapped up the acrylonitrile bottles in New Bedford MA, Coca-Cola apparently gave the go-ahead for commercial production in 1973. Monsanto quickly set up three factories to blow mold AN **Lopac™** bottles in three sizes, including the 10- and 16-ounce signature contour-shaped Coca-Cola bottles and a new wide-mouth 32-ounce generic bottle with flat sides for labeling.

Several years later after PET had become the material of choice and after Monsanto had shuttered their AN bottle plants, I met Mike Gigliotti (by the way, his son was a classmate of mine at Dartmouth's Thayer School of Engineering) and he confided to me that back in 1973 Coca-Cola had rejected the larger family-sized bottles which Monsanto had proposed to make from PET. He told me that Coca-Cola was focused on competing with PepsiCo in the small single service sized containers, which seemed odd to me, given that Coca-Cola was asking O-I to develop family-sized containers about that same time.

My conclusion was, and still is, that Monsanto and Coca-Cola both knew from those early consumer tests that AN could not be used safely to make family-sized containers, and that AN could not provide sufficient creep/thermal expansion resistance when used for carbonated soft drinks. However, Coca-Cola wanted so much to beat PepsiCo to the plastic bottle market that they were willing to go with Monsanto and with AN and small sized bottles.

Monsanto officially rolled out its **Cycle-Safe™** AN resin in 1975 and called the bottle the **EASY-GOER™**. Then it died! Monsanto had 100,000 of the 32-ounce bottles ready to hit the Chicago market in early 1977 when later that year the Food and Drug Administration stepped in to ban the bottle.

Explaining what happened gets complicated, but Gigliotti reportedly said that the issue stemmed from a turf battle between the FDA and the Environmental Protection Agency, then still a fledgling agency. The bitter battle between Coca-Cola and PepsiCo also apparently played a role.

The story goes that an environmental group sued the FDA over a test bottle that used Sohio's **Barex™** which also was an acrylonitrile-styrene copolymer modified with styrene-butadiene rubber (ABS). At the urging of the environmental group, the FDA issued a news release saying that chemicals migrating from **Barex™** "might someday" be found to be harmful.

Just that news release and the potential for an FDA issue was the death knell for all AN packaging.

Gigliotti claimed that Monsanto's AN **Lopac™** resin was different from Vistron's AN **Barex™** resin, but that claim was too little too late. **Lopac™** was also guilty by association.

Gigliotti said environmentalists began picketing supermarkets holding signs with Coca-Cola's slogan, *"Coca-Cola Brings Life to Your Party."* They had crossed out "life" and put a "Skull and Crossbones" and the word, Death, in its place!

Monsanto had no choice but to shutter its bottle factories in 1977, putting 800 people out of work, and that secured the opportunity for PET, especially in family-sized containers.

Gigliotti took early retirement and went on to co-found **TopWave™ Instruments Ltd.** which makes laboratory and testing equipment for plastic food and beverage containers, and he also started a consulting company, **MGA Inc**. which, by the way, collaborated with PTI on several consulting projects during our early days.

Ironically, seven years after killing it, the FDA approved the **Cycle-Safe™** bottle in 1984.

The agency said the bottle's acrylonitrile content had been reduced to safe levels, but Gigliotti claimed that the bottle was safe all along and that had the FDA earlier said publicly that nothing harmful could come out of the Monsanto bottle, the packaging world would have been different.

Things could have been different, and Mike Gigliotti is quoted as having said. "We could have made a beer bottle for less than a nickel."

As a trailer to this story about AN, I can't resist relating another "true" story which Paul Rothschild remembers and which may have spelled the end to AN as a resin for soft drink bottles, even without the FDA ruling. Apparently, the project manager for **Barex™** went on the TV program, "What's My Line," to tout the virtues of the new Sohio AN resin, **Barex™**. The panel did not guess what he did for a living, but as he explained that Sohio was developing a brand-new non-breakable plastic bottle for soft drinks, he pushed it off the table just to show that the bottle was unbreakable. But, when the camera zoomed in, the audience around the country saw a broken and leaking plastic soft drink bottle. Maybe that is really what killed the AN program for both Sohio and Monsanto, not the FDA ruling!

More About the Early Competition Between ANS and PET

This story is courtesy of Dr. Dan Weissmann, former Group Leader of Materials Development at Monsanto

Dr. Dan Weissmann

Dr. Dan Weissman lived "inside" the story of the competition between ANS and PET which offers additional inside perspective. He recalls, for example, that the notion that ANS was going to be the winner came about from the fact that during those early days, Coca-Cola was still asking for 2 years of shelf life because that's what glass bottles had always offered. However, all calculations showed that there was no way that PET could provide such a long shelf life in small containers, nor even in larger family-sized containers where the surface/volume ratio is much more favorable.

Dan also recalls that the realization that PET would eventually prevail came about in a meeting at Monsanto's Bloomfield offices in about 1976 when Monsanto's resident scientist, Dr. Sam Stingiser, was asked to carry out a comparison between ANS and PET for larger sized bottles. The emerging consensus after that analysis was completed was exactly what Mike Gigliotti had suggested, which is that no plastic bottle was going to offer 2 years of shelf life, regardless of size.

Part of the problem, however, was man made, as Dan recalls. Monsanto's design manager, Lars Shon, had determined that the production rates for preforms extruded and blown on dual cavity 18 station wheel machines with 36 cavities per wheel (15 of those wheel machine lines were already under construction!) would be the same for both the 32 and the 48 oz. bottles.

Dan, who was responsible for blowing the 48 oz bottles with just 8 months of blow molding experience (he joined Monsanto in April of 1973), quickly determined that the 48 oz preform which was 50% heavier than the 32 oz preform with all the additional weight added into the preform thickness was not going to work; blow molding resulted in frequent and unresolvable bottle blow-outs during the forming process.

In retrospect, Dan believes that a proper preform design could have solved the problem and that Monsanto could have developed larger sized ANS bottles. But it was too late to change designs, so Monsanto abandoned the commercialization of larger sized ANS bottles.

Dan also recalls that Monsanto did contract Professor Fred McGarry at MIT to oversee two programs at Monsanto, the first being Monsanto's effort to "simulate" the blow molding process on the computer. With very little data or expertise in utilizing a (then) very primitive version of blow molding computer simulation software and considering that they had to run only one simulation at a time with a turnaround time of one day, this effort was not able to help Monsanto solve their preform design issues. The other program that Dr. McGarry oversaw was a computerized thermal analysis of the "cool down" preform process from the melt temperature in the preform blow mold to a suitable blowing temperature with a conditioning step in the middle. However, that program also did not evolve quickly enough to impact the ANS blow molding issues.

Regarding the first choice of AN (acrylonitrile) material, Dan recalls that the early choice was methacrylonitrile-styrene (MS), code named MS-90, rather than acrylonitrile-styrene (ANS). MS-90 had much better thermal stability and color than did ANS.

Dan believes that the switch to ANS happened because AN was a product already manufactured by Monsanto while MS-90 was not. As it happens, AN is used to manufacture ABS (acrylonitrile-butadiene-styrene) which was already one of Monsanto's plastic products. Whether staying with MS-90 would have prevented the FDA issue, is still an interesting question.

Finally, Dan recalls that the residual AN monomer issue cited by the FDA was mainly due to the FDA's "Delaney Amendment" which demanded that no known carcinogen(s) could be added into the food chain. On the advice of Keller & Heckman in Washington, the Monsanto application was modified to expedite the approval, but ended up being considered under the food additives Delaney Amendment which, retrospectively, created a trap for Monsanto's FDA application.

Perhaps the final unfortunate circumstance for Monsanto was that because the FDA could not actually measure AN in any of the bottles, they asked Monsanto to develop a more sensitive test. Paradoxically, it was Monsanto who came up with a test procedure to detect AN at levels of only a few parts per billion, so Monsanto's own data was what the FDA used to disqualify AN for use in food packaging.

Ironically, the FDA later ruled that less than 6 ppb was equivalent to zero! As Dan concluded, "I guess life is full of what ifs."

The PET Decision

May 15, 1973   N. C. Wyeth, et. Al.   3,733,309
Biaxially Oriented Polyethylene Terephthalate Bottle.
Filed Nov 30, 1970

While the FDA's decision to disqualify AN for use in food contact applications was pivotal in the industry's move to PET, DuPont's expertise in the orientation of polyester for fiber and sheet applications was also a key factor. DuPont's research scientist, Nathaniel Wyeth, applied for and was granted US Patent 3,733,309 in 1973, which described how to make an oriented PET bottle, and which eventually paved the way for the commercialization of oriented PET bottles.

The Wyeth patent describes a process which involves molding a PET preform (a thick-walled close-ended tube) and then reheating, stretching, and blowing that preform into a bottle shape that is frozen in a blow mold cut to the bottle shape.

The plastic in the sidewalls of that final blow molded container becomes highly "oriented" and therefore offers the strength, impermeability, and drop impact resistance required to fabricate a functional soft drink container. Known today as stretch-blow molding, the process that Wyeth invented in the early 70's has become synonymous with the production of PET bottles.

RHB-5 Cincinnati Milacron Machine

While Wyeth's invention utilized PET preforms that were compression molded, today's PET preforms are injection molded in both one-stage (inject-cool-blow) and two-stage (inject-cool-reheat-blow) machine systems. It is also notable that DuPont also pursued the commercialization of PET by teaming up with Cincinnati Milacron and PepsiCo.

Cincinnati Milacron, a machine development and manufacturing company, developed the first two-stage reheat-stretch-blow molding machine, the RHB-4, and introduced that machine to the industry in 1976. Improved models of the machine were called the RHB-5, RHB-6, and RHB-7 and, as a byline to the story of the Milacron machine, I worked on site in Cincinnati with Milacron during the years 1976 to 1978 to help refine the RHB machine technology for O-I. In fact, I spent so much time in Cincinnati during the fall and winter one year that I joined a local adult basketball league in Cincinnati and played along with Bob Brazelton and the Milacron team!

Bill Gaiser and Broadway Mold in Dayton, Ohio, developed the injection mold for that first PET preform in 1973, and Broadway remained a well-respected mold supplier in the industry for many years.

Bill Gaiser

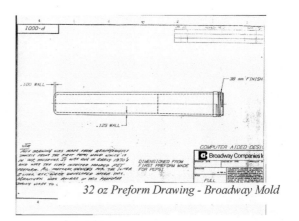

32 oz Preform Drawing - Broadway Mold

These developments culminated in the 1975 introduction of the first PET beverage bottle, a 32-oz PepsiCo container with a hemispherical bottom and with a separately injection molded PE base cup. That first bottle was molded by Amoco in Seymour, Indiana.

Early Amoco PET Bottles

The first non-beverage PET bottle for Scope mouthwash (46 oz), was also produced by Amoco, but not until 1979.

O-I, Continental, Sewell, and others followed quickly to design and produce many non-soft drink PET bottles for household chemical, food, and other beverage applications. In fact, by the early 1980's many former glass bottle applications had already converted to PET.

While Milacron's in-line reheat and blow technology dominated the PET bottle machine market throughout the 1980s, the one-step (inject-cool-blow) machine made its appearance in the U.S. in 1976 when Nissei of Japan sold three ASB machines to International Beverage Co. in Chicago to produce 64 oz and 32 oz PepsiCo bottles.

O-I partnered exclusively with Corpoplast of Hamburg Germany to commercialize the rotary reheat-stretch-blow molding machines (BAB-3 & BAB-4), also first installed and first used commercially in the US in 1976.

Corpoplast B-80 Rotary Reheat Stretch
Orientation Blow Molding Machine

Nissei Single Stage Cool and Blow
Orientation Blow Molding Machine

During those early years, several other companies also entered the plastic blow molding machinery market including Uniloy (eventually purchased by Johnson Controls and now part of Amcor), Van Dorn, and Jomar in the U.S.; Husky and Amsler of Canada; Sidel of France; Bekum, Corpoplast (now owned by KHS), and Krones of Germany; Automa, Magic, and SIPA of Italy; Aoki and Nissei of Japan; Mag-Plastic of Switzerland; and Urola of Spain.

It is worth noting, however, that O-I's decision to switch from AN to PET preceded the formal FDA ruling on AN but was influenced by a curious and unpleasant turn of events that also involved DuPont.

The sequence of events, as I recall them, started with the fact that O-I and DuPont had entered into a joint development agreement to explore both polyester (PET) and acrylonitrile (AN) as possible approaches, because both believed that they had to compete with Monsanto's proprietary **Lopac™** bottle which was already on the market.

Even though O-I's research was beginning to tell us that the best course of action might be a PET polyester bottle, our "development partner" (DuPont) kept telling us that they were convinced that Monsanto's acrylonitrile bottle approach was going to win the day.

In fact, DuPont had already trade-named their AN resin **Vicobar™** which stood for Victory Over Barex!

As it happened, however, while O-I executives Paul Rothschild and Randy Litten were meeting at DuPont with DuPont's Acrylonitrile Marketing Manager (his name escapes me), Paul happened to glance at correspondence upside down on his desk and noted a letter that was addressed to another Polyester Bottle Technical/Marketing group in DuPont which, as we eventually discovered much to our disappointment, had become DuPont's primary direction, and without acknowledging that to O-I.

Equally disappointing was our further eventual discovery that even as DuPont claimed to be working with O-I on this joint AN development project, they were also working jointly with Pepsi Cola and plastic blow molding machine manufacturer, Cincinnati Milacron, on the development of a manufacturing system to produce polyester (PET) bottles for PepsiCo.

After discovering the deception on DuPont's part, Bill Graham, VP and General Manager of the O-I Plastics Group, Bob Lanigan, O-I Corporate VP, and both Randy and Paul confronted DuPont's top executives about the deceptive way in which they had handled our O-I/DuPont joint technology development agreement.

It was not a friendly meeting and DuPont later sued O-I because they were afraid that O-I would challenge DuPont's Wyeth PET bottle patent, based on O-I's 1969 Scalora (US 3,470,282) patent which covered the orientation of PVC bottles. Tony Scalora was a retired O-I plastics expert who had obtained many patents then owned by O-I, including the PVC orientation process which, in principle, could be applied also to PET. The settlement was that O-I would not challenge the Wyeth patent and, in exchange, O-I would get a royalty free license to manufacture PET bottles. By the way, I was the Technical Expert in that lawsuit......what fun!

In any case, I do also recall that DuPont's contact at PepsiCo was a man named Jack Cahill who headed up the PepsiCo PET bottle development program, and who was also O-I's PepsiCo contact so, in retrospect, it was clear that DuPont knew everything we were doing with PepsiCo even when we thought we had separate confidential relationships with both PepsiCo and DuPont.

Understandably, that difficult experience forced us to re-focus O-I's efforts on developing a stronger relationship with Coca-Cola, which eventually led to our offering New York Coca-Cola exclusive lead-time incentives in exchange for O-I becoming the principal supplier to Coca-Cola on the East Coast.

As I recall, and prior to this experience with DuPont, we (O-I) were hoping to treat both PepsiCo and Coca-Cola as equal opportunity customers.

In any case, the move to PET by O-I was timely because we had just completed our Oriented Polymers Focused Effort and it was clear to those of us doing that work that PET was the material of choice, even though it had never been used previously for bottles, because it did not process anything like the conventional extrusion blow molding resins, including AN, PVC, PE, PP, and PS.

It turned out that accidentally reading that memo at the DuPont headquarters gave O-I an important jump-start in the race to develop a PET soft drink container, even though Amoco won the race to put the first PET bottle on the market.

However, Amoco was a raw material supplier with no packaging expertise and, predictably, Amoco did not pursue container manufacture once PET bottles were commercialized because Amoco was better positioned to make and sell terephthalic acid, a key chemical component used to make PET.

The Goodyear PET Resin Industry Story

This story is courtesy of Mr. Chuck Kern, retired Technical Associate who worked in the polyester/PET industry, first at Goodyear Tire & Rubber, then at Shell Chemical Company, and finally at M&G Polymers

Chuck and Mary Jo Kern

Goodyear began producing PET (polyester) in 1958 at its Point Pleasant WV plant. The plant initially made specialty copolyesters for a wide variety of applications including for use in textile fibers, coatings, and adhesives, but Goodyear also began producing PET homopolymer which was then "solid-stated" to raise the IV for conversion into tire cord at Goodyear's Alabama plant.

For the reader, IV stands for Inherent Viscosity and represents a simple way to define the molecular weight (average chain length) of the PET material. PET molecular weight can be increased by a process known as solid-stating which is simply cooking the PET at high temperatures under vacuum.

Higher molecular weight PET is stiffer during extrusion but has higher strength, better chemical resistance, and more resistance to degradation, which are properties important for both tire cord and for bottles.

Most PET products at that time were made "in-line," which means that raw chemicals were dumped into reactors where the PET chains were formed and then the polymer melt was delivered via melt pumps directly to dies either with tiny holes to form fibers or with long slits to form sheets.

Dupont made PET tire yarn the same way, in-line, but with higher IV PET to generate the higher strength via an in-line orientation/uniaxial stretching process.

Goodyear, however, may have been the first PET supplier to develop the solid-stating process, and as the world eventually discovered, solid-stating was a more economical way to produce high IV PET.

Goodyear's research also revealed that higher IV PET produces less acetaldehyde (AA) during melt processing, which is a requirement for bottles since AA, though harmless and nontoxic, can affect the taste of a beverage, even at very low concentrations.

Chuck also recalled that early in the PET bottle and resin development era, Goodyear continued to produce tire yarn but also bought tire yarn from DuPont and from other suppliers. Interestingly, Chuck said that DuPont was also buying some solid-stated PET from Goodyear, and as Chuck recalls, Goodyear had no idea what DuPont was doing with PET, but because the volume kept increasing, Goodyear finally figured out that DuPont was using Goodyear PET to develop the PET bottle process, since all of DuPont's PET capacity was being used in-line to make fiber and film.

Chuck also believes that DuPont was not interested in competing in the PET bottle resin business, nor in making PET preforms or bottles, because they did not have the solid-stating technology to economically increase the molecular weight, which at the time was required for bottles.

Chuck also noted that during this era Goodyear looked seriously at the possibility of going all the way from raw materials to preforms, but they also eventually abandoned that idea when it became clear that O-I and Continental were far ahead in developing proprietary processes to manufacture PET bottles.

About that same time Chuck recalls that Goodyear was building its first continuous polymerization line to supply the growing double knit fiber market which required a very pure PET so, as Chuck recalls, Goodyear also built a very high level of filtration into the PET plant design which, as it happens, was also required to make PET resin for bottles. By the time the new Goodyear fiber plant was commissioned, however, the double-knit fabric (remember leisure suits) was going out of style. So that brand new Goodyear plant was built to produce a fiber where there was no market, but fortuitously, that plant was also designed perfectly to produce the PET homopolymer that was then supplied to the Goodyear Scottsboro plant where it was solid-stated to a high 1.04 IV for use as tire yarn or to a lower IV for bottle applications. Goodyear's famous **Cleartuf 7202** PET resin was solid-stated only to .72 IV for 2-piece bottles. PET melt resin was batch solid-stated at the Goodyear Scottsboro AL plant early on and until continuous solid-stating capacity was added at the Point Pleasant plant.

Chuck recalls that once Goodyear was in the business of supplying bottle grade PET, they immediately set about developing what became Goodyear's famous **Cleartuf 7207** PET resin which had improved clarity and color over the **Cleartuf 7202** tire yarn polymer.

Chuck also recalls that Goodyear quickly developed copolymer PET resins 8006 (.80IV) and 8406 (.84IV) while working with Continental PET Technologies because the one-piece petaloid bottle required slightly higher IV to prevent stress cracking in the petaloid (footed) bottom. The copolymer formulation also helped with the processing of higher IV products in both injection and blow molding and with the new lighter weight preform designs that quickly emerged. As an added benefit, Goodyear learned that these new intermediate IV PET resins also worked well in Continental PET Technologies' heat set process which Continental had developed to make heat-resistant bottles for hot-fill juices.

O-I's PET development team also worked closely with Goodyear during those early days. We started up our Milford CT plant with Goodyear's high IV resins because we also wanted to prevent stress cracking in our two-piece base-cup bottle which had an elliptical bottom that was not so well oriented, to accommodate O-I's patented snap-on base cup. Goodyear supplied 90% of the market in those days, although competition came quickly from Celanese, Eastman, American Hoechst, and ICI.

Chuck also recalls that he had the opportunity to hear Nathanial Wyeth tell his story at the first SPE Blow Molding Division Technical Conference in 1983. Chuck says that while it was exciting to hear Wyeth tell of his discovery and the countless disappointments along the way, what he remembers most about Mr. Wyeth is that he told Chuck after introductions that "I wish I was a young man like you (Chuck was 34 at the time) because there is so much more that can be accomplished with PET containers."

Wyeth was already retired and knew he would not be a part of that upcoming excitement. And Wyeth was right. New applications and new technologies for PET packaging continued with new molding equipment developments, new packaging opportunities, and new resin developments.

Of course, all PET bottle producers had to pay a license fee to DuPont to use the DuPont patented **Dalar™** bottle making technology, but DuPont concluded that it would require significant capital to commercialize the new bottle process and they had other investment opportunities.

As the first significant PET bottle grade resin supplier, Goodyear assumed an early leadership position in developing new PET resin technologies. To help make this happen, in 1976 Goodyear established its own Bottle Applications Laboratory and equipped it with the first commercial Cincinnati Milacron laboratory blow molding machine (RHB-L) and they also added an injection molding machine to make preforms. This in-house capability allowed Goodyear to help customers start up their commercial processes and, as importantly, it gave Goodyear a window into better understanding the evolving polymer/processing relationships, which gave Goodyear important data for new resin developments.

Goodyear helped its customers to produce better bottles and Goodyear also provided training to its customers' operators and technical staff. Goodyear even developed a training seminar that was named "PET-101" and which I still have in my own old O-I files. In the early 1980's, bottle and machinery producers sought to reduce the cost of bottles by light-weighting and by increasing production rates. Weights for 2L one-piece bottles dropped from 67 gm to about 62 gm and injection molds of 16, 24, and 32 cavities replaced the early 8-cavity molds.

To help reduce bottle weights and increase throughput rates, Goodyear also helped lead the way by introducing new PET resins with a range of molecular weights (IV's) and with better consistency from batch to batch.

During the early 1980's, 2-liter bottles were introduced but were immediately under attack because of perceived non-recyclability and because brand owners wanted longer shelf lives for larger family-sized containers. Goodyear attacked the non-recyclability issue by introducing **REPETE™** which was the first-ever commercial 25% post-consumer recycle content PET.

During the late 80's, heat-set processes were developed to increase the thermal resistance of the containers so they could be filled at higher temperatures, a requirement for many of the fast-growing sport drinks such as Gatorade. Multi-layer technologies were also developed which allowed oxygen sensitive products such as ketchup to be packaged in PET. The new applications sometimes created new or additional resin requirements that kept the resin suppliers busy developing new grades, in addition to adding capacity.

Goodyear's development of a new high barrier PET copolymer, polyethylene naphthalate (PEN), put Goodyear in an early leadership position regarding the need for longer shelf life, although the eventual higher cost of PEN put the new resin out of reach for the commodity soft drink markets.

The Evolution of Goodyear's Polyester Business

1992 - Shell Acquires Goodyear's Polyester Business

From: United Press International Archives - The Goodyear Tire & Rubber Co. and the Shell Chemical Co. announced that Shell has agreed to buy Goodyear's polyester business. Included in the sale are Goodyear's polyester resin manufacturing facility in Point Pleasant, W.Va., the Goodyear Polyester Technical Center in Akron, and related assets. 'We are interested in acquiring the business because it holds a strong competitive position in a rapidly growing area,' Michael Grasley, president of Shell Chemical, said in a statement. 'Also, it will complement Shell's existing technology and feedstock capabilities.'

2000 – M&G Acquires Shell's Polyester Business

From: Independent Commodity Intelligence Services (ICIS) - Shell Chemical Company agreed to sell its polyethylene terephthalate (PET) resins business to Mossi & Ghisolfi (M&G) Group, an Italian PET converter in 2000. The purchase tripled M&G's annual sales to around $800 million. Shell's PET business comprised four plants having a total capacity of 610,000T per year, including units of 190,000T at Patrica, Italy, 30,000T at Glandford, England, 285,000T at Apple Grove, W.Va., and 105,000T at Altamira, Mexico. "M&G was one of Shell's major customers and was a joint venture partner with Shell's PET unit in Italy," said Neil Gaskell, chemicals portfolio task force leader at Shell.

Tom at a retreat with M&G, Goodyear, and Shell Executives and Customers

M&G, privately owned, was already one of Europe's largest manufacturers of pre-forms for PET bottles with an annual output of around 2.5 billion units, equivalent to 6 or 7 percent of the European market, and M&G's PET products accounted for two-thirds of M&G's annual sales of around $250 million, with a cellulose acetate operation making up the remainder. At the time, Guido Ghisolfi, M&G's vice-president of operations said, "We are fully committed to the PET sector, which we think has a profitable future despite its problems with overcapacity in the last two or three years."

The Eastman Chemical Company Story

This story is courtesy of Mr. Rod Broach, retired Eastman PET Sales Representative, including a 2018 Plastics News Magazine story documenting David Cornell's induction into the Plastics Hall of Fame

Tom Brady playing piano at an Eastman summer golf outing in 1990. Guests include TA Smith, Bill Young, Allen Rothwell, TJ Stevens, Bruce Larsen, Greg Nelson, our Guest Speaker, and several other guests.

The Eastman Chemical Company, a subsidiary of Eastman Kodak Company during the 1970's, was also a large producer of PET for the polyester fibers market, but Eastman's late entry into the PET bottle market during that period was predicated on having developed the first commercial "Green PET." Eastman began with a Spruce Green color and changed later to an Emerald Green color which both Coca-Cola and 7 Up had traditionally used for their Sprite and 7 Up soft drink products. These developments allowed Eastman to dominate the green PET market for many years.

Even though Eastman was late into the PET bottle market, the introduction of green PET opened the door for Eastman to also compete in the clear PET rigid packaging market, which eventually resulted in Eastman becoming the leader in supplying the emerging "extrusion grade" PET rigid packaging market with their trademarked **Eastar™**, **Spectar™**, and **Tritan™** copolyester resins.

Key players at Eastman during those years included Ed Denison, John Adams, Bill Gideon, Dave Cornell, TA Smith, and Rod Broach who was the first PET sales representative at Eastman and who for several years was responsible for the sale of Eastman PET resins for the entire world!

Playing golf at the Eastman summer golf outing in 1990. Guests include our speaker, TJ Stevens, Bruce Larsen, Bill Young, Allen Rothwell, Greg Nelson, Tom Brady, and several other guests.

Dave Cornell, a key business development representative at Eastman and one of the first Eastman employees to discuss the PET option with O-I in the early days of the industry, went on to play a major role in the emerging PET recycling markets and in 2018 was inducted into the Plastics Hall of Fame.

Plastics News Magazine, May 20, 2018

By Bill Bregar

David Cornell

Kingsport, Tenn. - David Cornell had a front-row seat in the early years of PET bottle development and plastics recycling. Now, Cornell is being inducted into the Plastics Hall of Fame.

He was the longtime technical director for the Association of Plastic Recyclers and had a 28-year career at Eastman Chemical Co. in Kingsport, where he still makes his home. He runs a consulting firm, DD Cornell Associates LLC.

Dave Cornell remembers the Garbage Barge of the late 1980s, searching for a home for New York's trash. He's an expert on life-cycle analysis. He palled around with famous garbologist William Rathje, an archeologist who dug through trash, proving that nothing degrades in a landfill. "Rathje was highly flamboyant. He would show up to give a talk in Levi's and a sports coat. He was a showman," Cornell said.

Cornell was on the scene in the first days of recycling. He was nominated to the Plastics Hall of Fame by Edward Socci, director of beverage packaging research and development for PepsiCo Inc.

"Dave Cornell is one of the giants of the plastics recycling industry," Socci wrote in his nomination. "Through his leadership, dedication, compassion and long service to the plastics recycling industry, Dave Cornell put the 'small town' of plastics squarely on the map." His efforts "helped to create the framework and arguments in support of plastics recycling," Socci said.

In high school, Cornell was more interested in metallurgy but got into biology when he got a grant from the National Science Foundation for a summer study of ecology at Denison University in Ohio. He attended the University of Delaware, earning bachelor's degrees in math and chemical engineering in 1969 and got a job at GE Aviation near Cincinnati as a materials engineer working on performance data and failure analysis for aircraft parts, including fire-protective coatings.

While at GE, he earned a master's degree in materials science from the University of Cincinnati and did a paper on the polymer polyoxymethylene (POM). Another project on PET led to a connection one of his professors had at Eastman Kodak Co. in Rochester, N.Y., and its Tennessee Eastman Co. in Kingsport.

Cornell eventually went to work for Eastman in 1973, becoming a PET pilot plant supervisor where he was put in charge of commercialization of the polyester business. He also held marketing and technical services positions.

While PET was developed for polyester fiber, it would be several years before PET bottles were commercialized.

Monsanto Co., in fact, created the first plastic soft drink bottle using polyacrylonitrile (Lopac™) resin, in 1975. The Cycle-Safe™ bottle held 32 ounces and Cornell said there was intense competition between Coca-Cola and PepsiCo to come up with large bottles, since glass was not acceptable for large size bottles. "What they concluded was that big bottles mean more sales. If we can sell more big bottles, we move more gallons," he said.

Coca-Cola and PepsiCo demanded a one-year shelf life and acrylonitrile passed that test but, unexpectedly, the Food and Drug Administration banned the material for bottles.

When DuPont got active in PET for soda bottles, Cornell said that DuPont planned to both sell the resin and make its own bottles, thereby competing with customers, which is why DuPont ended up canceling the project.

Coca-Cola and PepsiCo looked at both PVC and polyethylene as options, but those resins did not have the barrier properties needed for carbonated beverages, Cornell said, which left PET, and when the soft drink giants finally did some consumer testing, they found out they didn't really need a one-year shelf life. "So, over time, and this was the late 70s, the shelf-life requirement changed," Cornell said.

"PET, as it turned out, was cheaper than glass and optically clear, so the shorter shelf life prompted soft drink makers to streamline their distribution and get to market quicker. In fact, PET allowed the beverage companies to actually make more money, and soon, two-liter PET bottles were also on grocery store shelves," Cornell said.

At the same time, the U.S. polyester fiber business was under attack as clothing production moved to Asia, so Eastman officials asked: "What are we going to do with all this polyester polymer capacity, because it sounds like the party is closing down?" Cornell said.

Eastman's answer was to start up a PET reactor line in 1978 making green PET for 7-Up, which sold out quickly and helped Eastman's bottle-grade PET business grow by leaps and bounds," he said.

At the time, Cornell was the production manager for the group that made the PET polymers, so he had the opportunity to lead the development and commercialization efforts and to define specific resin formulations and manufacturing processes for making bottles, according to the Plastics Hall of Fame nomination.

The industry also began to look at the need for recycling in the late 1970s and early 1980s, according to Cornell, because it became obvious that "we were going to have an issue coming down the road about bottle deposit legislation passed back in 1978.

In 1987, the Garbage Barge grabbed headlines as it wandered the seas carrying more than 3,100 tons of trash from New York, searching for a home. The idea was to ship the trash to North Carolina, but officials there turned it back which was the stimulus that caused Rutgers University to start its Center for Plastics Recycling Research. Cornell represented Eastman as a founding member of the Center and took responsibility for rating project proposals for funding and for advising the center on technical and business realities.

Then came multimillion-dollar advertising campaigns by industry groups like the Council for Solid Waste Solutions, which tried to counter an anti-plastic sentiment in some parts of the country, and which had led to product bans. Cornell served on that technical committee as well.

Eastman was also a founding member of both the National Association for Plastic Container Recycling (NAPCOR) and The Association of Plastic Recyclers (APR) in 1987 where Cornell represented Eastman and played key technical roles.

In 1994, APR created the post of technical director, and named Cornell to the position. APR members were small independent entrepreneurs who were fierce competitors and as Cornell said, "These are owner-operators who might hock their wife's engagement rings to pay for the power bill, and who are dreamers on the one hand, but hard-headed as can be on the other."

He held that position at APR until he stepped back in 2015 to spend more time at home with his family.

PET is by far the most-recycled plastic and has a built-in market in the carpet industry, but Cornell knew early-on that new technologies would be needed to effectively recycle PET bottles, so he patented and developed systems for sorting dissimilar plastics as well as routes to chemically recycle PET where "We can take the polymer apart, and reassemble the raw materials and remake it," he said. Today, Cornell holds 15 patents in the fields of plastics and plastics recycling.

Cornell worked at Eastman until he retired in 2000, but he had played a big role in plastics recycling at a critical time for the industry. According to the Plastics Hall of Fame submission: "Prior to Dave's engagement, plastics were seen by many as an environmental blight, unworthy of public support. Plastics recycling was considered an impediment to the growth of the plastics industry. Through Dave's efforts, plastics recycling is now a mainstream commercial activity, helping to improve the health of the overall plastics industry and dramatically improving the industry's environmental impacts."

Cornell said people jumped into recycling in the early days and that the plastic lumber industry took off, but that many of those companies ended up failing. He recites what he calls his "standard speech" when he was asked for advice: "First question: Where are you going to get the raw material? Second question: What are you going to make? Third question: Do you have the process that gets the stuff you collect into the stuff you want to make? Fourth question: Do you have enough money to both build and operate your plant?"

"I've sung that song hundreds of times." Cornell said. "You've got to have value to drive recycling because recycling isn't a charity. If I can't make money, I'm not doing it," he said.

Cornell also led the creation of the APR *Design Guide for Plastics Recycling* and he created numerous testing protocols for plastic packaging recyclability.

Another of Cornell's major achievements was working with the Society of the Plastics Industry Inc. to provide the Food and Drug Administration with guidelines for recycled plastics in food-contact packaging. Those guidelines helped set the stage for FDA letters of nonobjection by recyclers.

Cornell was also at the forefront of the movement toward lifecycle analysis, the highly detailed study of a product's impact on the world, including the carbon footprint from production through transportation, recycling, consumer use, waste management, and water and energy consumption. "You have to do it if you want to get a holistic picture," he said.

In 1990, Cornell participated in a major weeklong workshop in Vermont with leaders from government, industry, environmental groups and from other disciplines to hammer out guidelines for how to conduct lifecycle analyses. The result was a book titled "*A Technical Framework for Life-cycle Assessment.*

He has also been active in plastics recycling issues at ASTM International and at the National Academy of Sciences.

Cornell analyzes data and writes the annual report on U.S. bottle recycling, a widely quoted document from APR and the American Chemistry Council. "My job is, first of all, to question the numbers to make sure they are consistent. I want to see trends. We do sanity checks. We do quality control," he said.

More than a dozen plastics recycling leaders endorsed Cornell for the Plastics Hall of Fame. APR President Steve Alexander called him "arguably one of the most influential voices in the history of the plastics recycling industry." His protocols and standards for recycling testing and design serve as the foundation of the industry, and he stands with the short list of industry giants in establishing, nurturing, and guiding the industry from development stage to its role today as a key contributor to sustainability and circular economy efforts worldwide," Alexander said.

O-I's Plastic Beverage Operations

Soon after the O-I Plastics Technology Development Team demonstrated the ability to manufacture a prototype 32 oz PET bottle, O-I's Executive Management Team created a new and separate O-I division for the purpose of developing the business of manufacturing and selling PET carbonated soft drink bottles commercially.

O-I named that new division Plastic Beverage Operations (PBO) and appointed a PBO Executive Team at an available building at the O-I West Technical Center on Westwood Avenue near the University of Toledo.

We jokingly called that PBO Headquarters building "The Little Red School House," because it was a small red brick building that looked for all the world like an old one-room schoolhouse.

Ken Ponsor, a former O-I glass executive who was a no-nonsense and get-it-done kind of executive, was appointed as the first General Manager of PBO in 1974.

Ken quickly filled out his executive management team, including Randy Litten as Director of Sales and Marketing and Paul Rothschild as Technical Director of Plastic Beverage Operations, although Paul also remained the Technical Director of the Plastic Products Division, so he wore two hats during that first year.

Jim Henry served as PBO's first Manufacturing Manager and Ron Watson was initially appointed Controller and Manager of Administration, but Jim McCornock replaced Ron when Randy Litten became General Manager of PBO in 1977.

Randy and Georgette Litten

Jim and Beth McCornock

Dick Roswech was recruited from the O-I Plastic Products Division plant in Cincinnati and was asked to manage the conversion of the former Aerosol Techniques (AT) metal aerosol container plant in Milford CT. O-I negotiated a long-term lease from AT in late 1974 and the PBO Milford CT plant became our (largest in the world) PBO Pilot Plant. We started up production of our first 32oz PET PepsiCo soft drink bottle at that PBO Milford plant in June of 1976.

Dick Roswech with his Thailand Family

I was responsible for the development of that first 32 oz bottle and remember "signing off" on using that bottle for use in a commercial application

Chuck Plymale

Along the way, O-I's Head of Plastics R&D, Chuck Plymale, who had watched O-I evolve as a leading glass container manufacturer, began declaring that he thought "the plastic soft drink bottle would never be successful." In fact, he reinforced that declaration, to his later despair, by saying early and often that he would "eat crow, if PET bottles ever became successful."

Well, you guessed the end to that story. In 1976 after successfully starting up the Milford Connecticut PET bottle operation, our entire management team gathered for dinner at the Westgate Hotel near the O-I Technical Center and we invited Chuck Plymale as the guest of honor ..... to eat a carefully prepared (real) crow for dinner! I am delighted to report that Chuck, literally, had to "eat his words," but also that he did so with the best of humor and, thereafter, became a huge supporter of the Plastic Beverage Operations!

Paul Rothschild, by the way, remembers that O-I R&D VP, Bob Santelli, told him that he would "kiss Paul's ass in Macy's window if PET ever became commercial." Perhaps fortunately, Dr. Santelli passed away before Paul could collect.

However, Paul also recalls the trailer to that story which is that when Ken Ponsor, Randy Litten, and Paul were appointed to run the **PBO** PET commercialization operation, they were told that they were "second" into the revolving door (assuming failure) and that they needed to "come out first."

My first O-I Executive Office

Returning to the PBO story, I was appointed Technical Director of PBO in 1977 and Paul Rothschild resumed his full-time role as VP and Technical Director of the Plastic Products Division.

After Randy Litten assumed the PBO General Manager's role in 1977, he quickly appointed John Bachey, a

John and Elaine Bachey

former O-I **Hi-Cone™** Carrier Product Manager, to replace him as the PBO Marketing and Sales Manager. John and I, by the way, travelled frequently together to meet with customers during those early years and we kept a continuous gin rummy game going for our airline flights. As you can imagine, John and I have very different memories of who won that grand competition!

Dewey Longstreet

In quick succession, John Bachey and Randy Litten hired Dewey Longstreet, George Boucher, and Paul Meyer to handle Customer Service. Paul Meyer created a nationwide Customer Service force including Ludy Kagoy in Birmingham AL, Don Saloff in Milford CT and Walt Rupley in Toledo. John Bachey assembled a national sales force during that 1977 to 1980 period which included Bob Staats in Milford CT, Jack Ardrey in East Brunswick NJ, Bob Henning in Havre de Grace MD Hank Powell in Birmingham AL, and Neal Boden in City of Industry CA.

Ken Scheurmann, a former Plastic Products Division plant manager, was appointed Manufacturing Manager for PBO, reporting to Randy Litten. Ken Scheurmann eventually moved to Havre de Grace MD to manager PBO's second manufacturing plant at which time Chris Gimre moved over from O-I's TV Products Division to replace Ken Scheurmann.

As we rolled out additional plants, Dick Morrette got Birmingham AL, Dick Voss managed East Brunswick NJ, and Jim Henry managed the City of Industry CA plant.

Randy Litten, by the way, recalls trying to hide the expenses which he had to approve for moving Jim Henry's horses (Jim was not only an All-American point guard for Vanderbilt University during his college years but he and his wife were also devoted horse riders and trainers!) from Toledo to City of Industry, and then back again when Jim was replaced by Bruce Johnson.

All of this happened over a 3-year period from 1975 to 1977.

Robert Schad

Also, during this PBO startup period and beginning several years prior to and during the technology development phase, the O-I Plastics Products Division Management Team, led by Paul Rothschild, in cooperation with the Plastics Technology Management Team, led by Greg Fehn, negotiated exclusive development and equipment supply agreements with Husky Injection Molding Systems of Toronto Canada and Corpoplast GMBH from Hamburg Germany.

Husky, founded by Robert Schad, was a leader in the supply of injection molding equipment but needed the hot runner technology developed by the O-I Technical Team to design injection molds and systems that would process PET into preforms. In exchange for providing O-I's injection processing technology, Husky agreed to become the exclusive supplier of preform injection molding equipment to O-I's Plastic Beverage Operations.

Corpoplast GMBH, a spinoff from Germany's Gildemeister Group, was the first company to develop a rotary reheat-stretch-blow molding machine capable of making reproducible bottles at high speed, which was a requirement for the economical production of carbonated soft drink bottles that could compete with glass and metal.

Gunter Kleimenhagen, R&D Manager at Gildemeister, helped manage the spinoff of Corpoplast from Gildemeister GMBH, and he was soon named the General Manager of the new spinoff company, Corpoplast.

Gunter told me that as early as 1968, Heidenreich and Harbeck (H&H) produced the very first biaxially oriented plastic bottle. That first oriented bottle was made from PVC for beer, and on the very first reheat-stretch-blow molding machine.

This new development sparked the interest of converters, resin companies, and bottlers around the world, not just in Europe.

Gunter Kleimenhagen

And this new machine development by H&H also created the opportunity for Mr. Kleimenhagen to meet with O-I's Plastic R&D Team led by Jim Heider, although PET and soft drink bottles were not yet even in the picture.

Gunter told me that this first contact between O-I and H&H led O-I to schedule a visit to H&H in Hamburg Germany, just to evaluate this new bottle orientation machine. That first visit included several of O-I's top executives, Sr. Executive VP, Malcom Cooper and Plastic Products Division Technical Director, Paul Rothschild. The O-I Executive Team met with Gunter, as well as with Horst Klemme, Gunter's boss.

O-I's interest in this new technology was, in part, what encouraged Corpoplast in 1970 to develop a first prototype reheat-stretch-blow molding production machine that could produce an incredible 10,000 1/3-liter bottles per hour. This first prototype machine, called a BA2, was used to make test market quantities of 1/3-liter beer bottles that were filled and tested at local breweries. Gunter told me that the success of that first project encouraged Corpoplast to also evaluate both **Barex™** and **Lopac™** as options for improved barrier properties.

In 1971, Corpoplast signed a confidentiality agreement with DuPont's Dr. Sroog for the purpose of evaluating a proprietary DuPont bottle resin. Gunter recalls that DuPont used a code name for that resin and did not reveal the material composition, but that experimental resin must have been a specialty version of PET, either a copolymer or a homopolymer with a different molecular weight.

Karl Seifert

Gunter also recalls that Mr. Nyquist from DuPont was sent to Hamburg to stay for several months and to work with Corpoplast engineers Otto Rosenkranz and Karl Seifert (their names are on the early Corpoplast machine patents) on the Corpoplast lab equipment, where both extruded tubes and injection molded preforms were tried, and while using three grades of DuPont's "proprietary material."

Based on the results of these early trials, Corpoplast built its first BAB-3 machine in 1972 which could produce 7,000 1.5-liter bottles per hour, and which was the precursor for the first BAB-3 (1975) designed to specifically manufacture PET bottles at DuPont's Wilmington, Delaware plant, managed by Mr. Houle, and for PepsiCo, at the direction of Jack Cahill and Al Alberghini.

Corpoplast BAB-3 Machine

In 1974 Corpoplast entered into an agreement with O-I for exclusive sales of Corpoplast blow molding machines in the USA, except for DuPont and Pepsi Cola, who already had an agreement with Corpoplast.

For that reason, a joint company was formed here in the US, officially named Corpoplast, Inc. USA, and was headed by Jim Henry of O-I as General Manager.

Later, this agreement was dissolved by Corpoplast because O-I declined to market those machines except to O-I's own operations.

Corpoplast BAB-4 Machine

Bottles made by O-I using Corpoplast and Husky machines

O-I did purchase a second BAB-3 machine but, thereafter, asked Corpoplast to develop a new machine designed for 2-liter soft drink bottles, with a lower output. That machine was named the BAB-4.

Peter Rose of Corpoplast provided a very nice chronology of the O-I/Corpoplast commercial relationship during the 5-year period (1974-1979) when O-I established itself as a competitive force in the emerging PET bottle industry, employing Corpoplast rotary blow molding machine technology.

Chronology: Corpoplast - North & South America.			Page: 1
Updated: By Peter Rose; Sen. Technical Manager; June-2000.			
File: D:\Daten\Excel-00\Chonology.USA			
Pos.:	Date:	Events:	Key-Players:
1.	Dec.-1974	Processing of the first O.-I. PET-Preformes on the BAB-3 in Hamburg, after the Dupont acceptance run.	O.-I.: G. Fehn, R. Morrett, A. Dickson, Tom Brady. Gildem.: G. Kleimenhagen, P. Rose, O. Rosenkranz.
2.	June-1974	Joint venture: Gildemeister AG & Owens-Illinois. See Wallstrett Journal information, June-21/1974.	O.-I.: M. Cooper, K. Ponsor Gildem.: H. Klemme & G. Kleimenhagen.
3.	Jan./Feb.-75	Installation and operation of the 1-st. BAB-3 for the production of 2.0-ltr. Pepsi-PET-Bottles. Customer: Dupont. 30x Mold -Stations Capacity: 6000 PET-Bottles per hour.	Dupont: G. Houle. Pepsi: Keyhill, A. Alberghini. Gildem.: P. Rose, H.Conow. B. Kobelentz.
4.	1975	USA-Corporation: Gildemeister Corpoplast & Owens Illinois.	Vice-President: Jim Henry. Gildem.: H. Klemme & G. Kleimenhagen.
5.	March 1975	1-st. Project meeting with Owens Illinois in Toledo.	O.-I.: P. Rothshield, G. Fehn, A. Dickson, Tom Brady. Corpopl.: O. Rosenkranz & P. Rose.
6.	May-5/1975	The shape of the PET-Preform is defined by O.-I.	O. I.: Tom Brady.
7.	June - July 1975	Installatioln of the BAB-3 at the Owens Illinois plant of Milford /Connecticut. Product: 1.5-ltr. Pepsi-PET-Bottle. Capacity: 6000 PET-Bottles per hour. 30x Molding -Stations	O.-I.: R. Roswech, Plant-Manager, Andy Dickson. John Walsh, Jim Berry. Gildemeister Corpoplast: Peter Rose; Field Manager. H. Conow, B. Kobelentz, K. Krause.
8.	Oct.-1976 until June-1977	Major improvements of the BAB-3: Lapping procedure for the distributor plates. Honeing procedure to improve the stretching of the preforms. Inspection of the air-flow ratio of the stretch-rod. Fixing of the Maltees Cross. Preplacement of the preform feeding device. Improving of the gear train: "The halve moon is risen". Closing of the gear train by the "last key-gear".	O.-I.: Henry Pinto & John Walsh, Jim Berry, Lilly Pad, John Miclos "Glue Bear". R. Roswech "Big Bear". Corpopl.: P. Rose & Otto Rosenkranz, K. Krause.
9.	June-1977	Installation of the 1-st. BAB-4 (2200 bph). Owens Illinois plant of Milford / Connecticut. 6x Molding -Stations	O.-I.: Henry Pinto & John Walsh, John Miclos. P. Rose; Field Manager.
10.	July-1977 until Dec.-1978	Major improvements of the BAB-4: Redesign of the entire stretch-unit. Seating of the preforms. Procedure to align the "Horse-Head" together with the "Eyes of the Bull". Securing of the mandrel transfer. Development of the water cooled cooling shields.	O.-I.: R. Roswech, Big Bear Henry Pinto & John Walsh, John Miclos "Glue Bear". O.-I./Toledo: Andy Dickson & Nick Curto ("Black Bear"). Corpl.: P. Rose.
11.	1978 until 1979	In total are 10x BAB-4's installed at the O.-I./Plant of Mildford.	O.-I.: R. Roswech; Plant-Manager. Corpl.: P. Rose.

Peter Rose and Scott Steele

I should also give proper recognition to Scott Steele, the O-I Senior Engineer who became O-I's, and then PTI's, blow molding process expert, under the tutelage of Peter Rose!

As happened with Husky, O-I offered its PET blow molding process technology to Corpoplast in exchange for commercial blow molding machine exclusivity in the US and, it is important to note that the key technology contributed by O-I was Andy Dickson's US patent 4,247,487 which covered the concept of blowing cooling air onto the outside of the preform while heating it with near infrared radiation.

While Dickson's patent was later ruled invalid because others had previously used this technology to heat hams, Dickson's patent nevertheless turned out to be the key to making high production reheat blow molding machines, and Dickson's patent served as the basis for O-I's contractual relationship with Corpoplast. As a result, O-I began the PET bottle business in 1976 with exclusive and, at the time, superior preform injection and orientation blow molding technologies from both Husky and Corpoplast.

Andy Dickson, Mr. Physiker, Tom. Brady, Dick Morrette, Greg Fehn, Otto Rosenkranz

The Plastic Beverage Operations Technical Center

The PBO headquarters building, i.e., "The Red School House," was located just south of the O-I Technical Center at what was then known as the O-I Development Center which had been used by O-I for the purpose of creating pilot manufacturing operations for all the O-I divisions. Once the technical development of new PET bottle technologies had been completed at the O-I North Technical Center, it was logical to move the PBO technical development activity entirely into the O-I Development Center.

After the official creation of the Plastic Beverage Operations business unit, that's exactly what happened.

Even during the development stages of the project, our pilot scale injection and blow molding machinery had already been located in what used to be O-I's metal can plant at the Development Center, but once the Red School House became the PBO Headquarters, we moved the entire PBO technical operation to the Development Center and we also created a machine tool center where we could quickly manufacture or modify equipment and molds.

Greg Fehn who had managed the process development activities up until our move to the Development Center opted to remain with the O-I Plastics R&D effort, and he moved back to the O-I North Technical Center. Saleh Jabarin also remained with O-I Corporate Plastics R&D to manage the continuing materials development function.

I chose to officially transfer from O-I Corporate R&D into the fledgling O-I Plastic Beverage Operations Division as the PBO Technical Director and I assumed responsibility for all the technical commercial development activities which had been relocated to the O-I Development Center.

Dr. Long Fei and Tommie Chang

One of my first (and I might even say "brilliant") moves was to ask Dr. Long Fei Chang to join us full time at PBO. Long Fei had previously been a Senior Associate in the O-I Computer Science Department and I first met Dr. Chang while I was engaged in the O-I Oriented Polymers Focused Effort. However, I soon discovered that Long Fei had a PhD in Electrical Engineering, had taught Applied Math, and that he also had a talent for taking massive amounts of experimental data and creating algorithms that could predict the behavior of plastics in processing machinery.

Perhaps my greatest contribution to the eventual commercial success of PBO was simply to recognize back in the early 1970's that Long Fei's talent for computer simulation and design was exactly what we needed to understand and predict the behavior of this new and unique PET material that could exist in both the amorphous and crystalline states, was subject to almost instant hydrolytic degradation under even normal plastic processing conditions, generated acetaldehyde during hydrolytic degradation (a harmless chemical compound found in many fruits, but one that could affect the taste of a beverage or food product at levels of just a few parts per million), was commercially producible at various molecular weights and with several polymer chemistries, and was ultra-sensitive to property changes as a function of biaxial orientation.

Several of us in the O-I Corporate R&D Laboratories had generated massive amounts of experimental processing, property, and performance data for many of the polymers used for packaging, including PET, and over a wide range of processing and end-use conditions. But almost by happenstance we discovered that Long Fei could correlate all of this data using his algorithms to not only predict injection and blow molding processing conditions but also to actually predict final material distributions, degrees of orientation, and therefore the final shelf life and performance of a blow molded and oriented PET container.

His algorithms, as it turned out, could also be used to dimension the very sensitive preform design(s) that were necessary to achieve these container performance results, which is how we learned that every different bottle design requires a different preform design, if we wished to achieve optimum container performance.

Today, we take computer simulation and design almost for granted, but in those days, Long Fei's algorithms were created using FORTRAN, which is now considered to be primitive software.

In fact, much of the "technology transfer" we offered to both Husky and Corpoplast in exchange for mold and machine exclusivity back in the mid 1970's was based on the algorithms that Long Fei had developed for both injection and blow molding processing, something that no one else in the industry had yet developed or had access to.

The trailer to that story is that after retiring from both O-I and the University of Toledo Polymer Institute, Long Fei Chang joined our team at PTI where he stimulated the development of our proprietary "Virtual Prototyping" software that still makes PTI the industry leader in computer-aided design and simulation of plastic molds, machines, preforms, and containers!

And the trailer to that story is that at an advanced age, Long Fei is still working part time at PTI!

In addition to Long Fei Chang, I would be remiss not to remember and recognize the unsung contributions of several other important researchers in the O-I corporate research laboratories who contributed to our fundamental understanding of the polymer chemistry and physics that were critical to our eventual design of and successful manufacture of the PET bottle.

Dr. Santos Go and Dr. Lynn Taylor published an important internal O-I research study and review of the degradation processes of polyesters, including the plausible and known mechanisms for thermal, oxidative, and hydrolytic degradation of PET. Rereading this 1975 historic document reminds me that the early fundamental chemistry work done at O-I was critical to our eventual commercial success.

I must also pay tribute to Dr. Go's research colleagues, Dr. Eugene Welsh, Dr. David Weinberg, James Brug, Fred Cassidy, Dr. Ernie Lippert, Dr. Wendell Kollen, Dr. Bob Fechter, Tom Marino, Bill Bayer, Dennis Balduff, and Jim Crawford who also contributed essential knowledge to O-I's fundamental understanding of the chemistry and physics of both AN and PET, and of all the competing packaging plastics.

Back in 1975, I also hired John Tobias to manage our first PBO Quality Control Laboratory. John had a long history of lab testing experience at O-I, and he also had experience with taking products from the lab to the field, so he was the right choice for that time in the commercial development. In fact, John set up virtually all the quality control laboratories in our PBO plants over a 4-year period.

Eventually, as we created those four PBO plants across the country and as we added even more sophisticated quality control and testing regimes, I asked Dr. Jim Fargher to join our effort and to manage our combined PBO Analytical Testing and Quality Control

John and Mary Jo Tobias

Laboratories. Jim also had a long history with O-I and had, in fact, worked in the O-I Corporate Analytical Laboratory when our Polymer Materials and Processing Group asked Jim and his colleagues, including Dr. Frank Schloss, to develop several of the analytical test methods that we were using then, and indeed continue to use today, for quality control in our PET container plants.

As I said previously, the natural degradation product of PET is a compound called acetaldehyde (AA) which is a harmless natural flavorant in fruits

Jim and Suzy Fargher

such as bananas, and as one might expect because it is a flavorant, even small residual quantities of AA (in the parts per million range) in a PET bottle sidewall can migrate into a beverage and change the taste of that beverage, perhaps not for the average consumer, but for the "super tongue taste testers" at Coca-Cola and PepsiCo.

So controlling processing conditions during the manufacture of a PET preform and bottle is absolutely essential and during our early work on PET processing technologies Dr. Fargher was the O-I Senior Analytical Chemist who along with Dr. Frank Schloss, also an O-I Senior Analytical Chemist, developed the methods for determining quantities of AA in commercial PET preforms and bottles and which, as I said, became industry standard testing methods that are still used routinely in the industry.

Frank and Willma (Bingo) Schloss

Interestingly, to employ Dr. Fargher's test methods as quality control tests, we also had to "predict" the quantities of AA that might migrate into a beverage or food product after filling and, you guessed it, the person who created algorithms to accurately predict migration as a function of shelf life, storage temperature, humidity, processing conditions, and material properties was Dr. Long Fei Chang!

So, thanks to Drs. Chang and Fargher and Schloss, O-I developed, and eventually gave to the industry, the most critical PET preform/bottle quality control test that is still used today!

My contribution, I am proud to say, was hiring them and then "getting out of their way!"

Another important and early addition to our PBO Technical Development Team was Andy Dickson, another experienced O-I corporate R&D engineer with many years of machine and process development experience.

Andy joined our team as Manager of Process Development and not only led the development of new container forming machinery and equipment but also worked with our injection and blow molding equipment suppliers to convert their conventional plastics processing technologies to handle PET.

Other experienced plastics engineers who worked closely with Andy and who had done much of the early R&D work in Corporate Research included Wolfe Bode, Nick Curto, Jim Herman, Mike Cameron, John Kidwell, Dick Morrette, Dave Beekley, and Jim Foote.

Bob Kontz, Jim Gearig, and Frank Patek handled our product and machine design activities and Bob Kontz was a genius at conceiving of and designing, from scratch, new and untested machinery. Bob designed what eventually became our "go to" unit cavity PET preform injection machine. We built several and ran them almost continuously in our process laboratory and we called them "The Kontz Machines."

Bob Kontz also designed and patented the previously mentioned base cup application machine that became the standard in our Milford CT plant when we couldn't get commercially available machines to work properly.

Al Uhlig

Another genius designer/inventor who worked closely with us was Albert Uhlig. Albert was the inventor of many products and processes over the years at O-I and his name is on hundreds of patents. Al Uhlig's patents cover cap and closure concepts, a new "Impact Injection Process" and the "Cool and Blow" Extrusion Blow Orientation Process, which was eventually commercialized by Bekum, under license to O-I.

We built most of this custom-designed machinery in our building in our own machine shop that was run by another genius tool and die machinist, Bill Graybill. Without Bill Graybill and Bob Kontz and Al Uhlig, we might never have commercialized our first base cup bottle design in Milford CT.

PVC Cool and Blow Orientation Machine

Perhaps even more important to our development effort during those years were our process lab technicians and junior engineers including Gary Hager, Jeff DeGross, Wayne Schall, John Feick, Prakash Ajmera, Bob Burmeister, Jim Berry, Butch Bundy, Oliver Brownridge, Roy Swantusch, Glen Ver Hage and Jim Twigg, who not only ran our prototype base cup application, pipe extrusion, orientation blow molding, and injection machines, but who also helped start up our Milford, Havre DeGrace, Birmingham, City of Industry, and East Brunswick manufacturing plants.

I unfortunately don't have photographs of our entire team but to help close the loop, I am including several random old photos that I had hidden away, and which offer a perspective on the "hands on" dedicated team that we put together in those days!

Albert Uhlig

Long Fei Chang

Gary Hagger

Mike Cameron

Andy Dickson

Jim Fargher

Frank Patek

Jim Gearig

Jim Herman

John Kidwell

Oliver Brownridge

Wolfe Bode

"Relaxing After Work"

Jeff DeGross

O-I's Milford Connecticut "Pilot Plant"

I put "Pilot Plant" inside quotation marks because, although it was intended initially to be a pilot plant, the Milford plant quickly became a massive 24/7 production plant with almost all experimental equipment, and PBO management asked Dick Roswech to not only manage that plant but also to work with our O-I engineering teams to test and develop the new equipment, and he was expected to make production quotas for PepsiCo on experimental and developing production equipment.

In retrospect, the expression we use today, "Building the airplane as we fly it," really did fit the Milford plant.

While only a few of the technical team members in Toledo moved permanently to become part of Dick Roswech's staff, including Tom Francis, John Johnson, Dick Morrette and John Kidwell, many of us and many of the Corpoplast and Husky technical support personnel spent days, weeks, and even months living in the Holiday Inn in Milford as we worked to make those experimental production machines run.

Peter Rose

Corpoplast BAB-3 Machine in Production

I can remember working 14-hour days in the plant with Peter Rose from Corpoplast and with Andy Dickson and then retiring to the Holiday Inn where we played tennis together under the lights on a nearby tennis court, at night!

I also remember Peter and me positioning ourselves for hours on either side of the massive BAB-3 rotary blow molding machine and yelling instructions to each other as we tried to optimize the infrared reheating system, designed and patented by Andy Dickson, so that Dick Roswech could meet the next PepsiCo order!

I also recall spending hours and hours on the floor with Bob Kontz, Nick Curto, Andy Dickson, Henry Pinto and John Bombace trying to optimize the base cup application machines which required the application of a snap-on base cup to a sometimes not-so-exact blow molded bottle bottom, and we also had to apply glue using those base cup application machines while we positioned our 2-liter spherical-bottomed bottle in an injection molded polyethylene base cup and tried to make all those bottles "perpendicular!"

We introduced more than just the Husky, Corpoplast, and Kontz Base Cup machines into Milford because we were trying to arrive at longer term solutions for all the manufacturing process steps and because other companies were developing competitive options for each of those manufacturing processes.

43

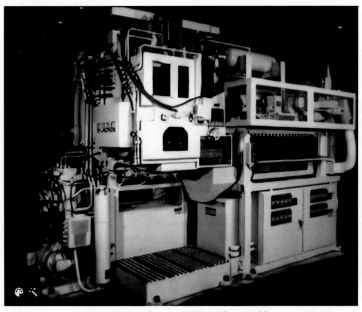

Cincinnati Milacron RHB-5 Blow Molder

We tried Stokes rotary-platen injection molding machines to make preforms and we tried several different injection machines, including models from Van Dorn and Husky, to make the polyethylene base cups. We also added Cincinnati Milacron RHB-4, RHB-5 and RHB-7, reheat-stretch-blow-molding machines and we tried Nissei single stage injection-stretch-blow machines.

One of the intractable problems we ran into with the Stokes injection machines was that they periodically produced preforms with "cracked finishes" (finish is the technical term for the threaded portion of the bottle opening). We worked for months to find a set of processing conditions that would eliminate the cracked finish problem, but we finally abandoned the Stokes machine as an option because we just could not sustain quality production on those machines.

We had one of almost every type of developmental machine installed at Milford, and at one point about a year into the project, Dick Roswech had more than 400 hourly workers to man all 3 shifts, mostly to fix machinery and to physically fix line issues so that he could keep the manufacturing lines running.

However, I am happy to say that back then we were all young enough and inexperienced enough that we didn't really know that we were trying to "build the airplane as we flew it!"

And with the dedicated help of the Toledo technical team and the terrific staff that Dick Roswech hired including John Johnson, Tom Francis, Henry Pinto, John Bombace, Dick Morrette, John Kidwell, and with the help of the customer service crew led by Paul Meyers and the sales team led by John Bachey and Bob Staats, Milford very quickly became a terrific success in O-I's emerging Plastic Beverage Operations container business.

Beyond Milford CT

After our early success and learnings at the Milford CT plant which was supplying New York Coca-Cola, one of the most demanding customers on the planet, PBO Management got approval to create additional manufacturing operations in Havre de Grace MD, City of Industry CA, and Birmingham AL.

Ken Scheurmann started up the Havre de Grace plant. Jim Henry started up the City of Industry plant. Dick Morrette started up the Birmingham plant, and in 1982 Dick Voss started up and ran a fifth PET bottle manufacturing operation inside the O-I East Brunswick NJ Plastic Products Division plant.

Dick Voss hired another young engineer out of our technical team at O-I, Doug Wehrkamp, who eventually moved with Dick Roswech to start up the 2nd Coca-Cola self-manufacturing plant in Ashville NC.

By the early 1980's O-I had several viable competitors including Continental PET Technologies (eventually acquired by O-I), Sewell (eventually acquired by Dorsey and then Constar), Amoco (eventually acquired by Silgan), and Johnson Controls (eventually acquired by Amcor).

However, and perhaps in retrospect, O-I was positioned to lead, perhaps even dominate, the fledgling PET plastic bottle industry, because O-I had proprietary access to the only high-speed rotary blow molding technology via the agreement with Corpoplast.

O-I also had proprietary access to the most advanced PET preform injection machine technology via the agreement with Husky and O-I had the chance to leverage its dominance and sales position in the glass bottle business which serviced the same food and beverage brand owners domestically and internationally.

In addition, O-I owned and operated a separate bottle cap and closure division, and O-I was also a leader in the polyethylene and PVC plastic bottle businesses which also served those same brand owners.

Had O-I understood the strategic opportunity of leveraging its dominance in the packaging world by having the Plastic Products Division, the Plastic Beverage Operations, the Closure Division, the Component Products Division, and the Glass Container Division all collaborate to serve the major food and beverage brand owners, which none of O-I's competitors could have done, O-I could have dominated the emerging PET plastic container business. Instead, O-I began to see the PET bottle as a threat to its historic glass bottle business and in 1984 decided to abandon any further expansion of the PET bottle business.

The End of PET at O-I

I got my first real message from O-I management that the success of the PET beverage bottle was a threat to all of O-I's other packaging businesses when, as Technical Director, I explored several other related PET packaging opportunities which were summarily rejected by O-I without any substantive analysis or consideration. Perhaps I was young enough and naive enough not to be discouraged by those rejections, but in retrospect, both of those opportunities could have cemented O-I's dominance in what quickly became a once-in-a-lifetime industry opportunity.

The first opportunity came when my counterpart, the Technical Director of Wilson Sporting Goods, called me one day and asked for a meeting. As it turned out, he wanted to ask whether O-I was interested in helping Wilson develop a plastic tennis ball can. Recall that every tennis ball can in the world at that time was metal. I, of course, said "yes" and promised to get back to him with a development plan, but when I took the idea to my O-I management, they summarily rejected the proposal and told me that putting tennis balls in a plastic can would never fly (no pun intended).

Well, my new Wilson Technical Director friend was disappointed, but the very next day he called O-I's number one competitor, Continental (Can) PET Technologies, and asked them the same question.

As they say in the movies, "The rest of the story is history!" Continental said "yes" to Wilson's request and within three years there was not a metal tennis ball can on the planet, and guess who was making them? O-I's number one competitor, Continental.

That is a tough story for me to tell, especially about my own company at the time, but it is a true story, and in my mind, could have changed the course of O-I's plastic packaging history.

My second story is equally difficult for me to tell. Not long after the Wilson Sporting Goods opportunity passed, I received a call from Mel Druin, a senior executive at the Campbell Soup Company who wanted to talk to O-I about helping Campbell convert from metal frozen dinner trays to plastic trays, and specifically, Campbell wanted to use crystallized PET (CPET) because crystallized PET resists softening at oven reheat temperatures and would potentially be recyclable and might represent a modern addition to Campbell's frozen dinner lines that at the time were all packaged using aluminum trays.

After several preliminary discussions, I learned that what Campbell really wanted was for O-I to develop and manufacture CPET trays for Campbell, another opportunity for O-I to leverage its PET and package manufacturing knowledge and to develop a whole new product line.

Again, I presented what seemed like another interesting product opportunity to my O-I management, and again the idea was summarily rejected as something that was well outside O-I's container manufacturing DNA.

I was again disappointed, but like a good company soldier, I relayed O-I's answer to Mel and to others at Campbell, including Ed Bauer, a senior technical manager at Campbell.

Mel was surprised and disappointed because Campbell really was not interested in manufacturing their own packaging. However, Mel and Ed Bauer called me again to ask whether O-I would at least be interested in helping Campbell to set up its own CPET tray self-manufacture operation on a paid project basis.

When I presented that to O-I management, they were happy to agree since a paid project would produce revenue and O-I would not have to assume any apparent new product risk. So, we signed an agreement to assist Campbell. I asked Bob Deardurff to become the Campbell project manager and to manage the entire CPET tray manufacturing installation project in California.

To Campbell's benefit, Bob agreed and moved his family to California for the better part of a year to make that happen for Campbell.

O-I was paid well for handling the project and Bob not only learned a lot but was recognized by Campbell management when the line was up and running, for doing an outstanding job.

So, while the Campbell CPET tray project was a success and while O-I did another great job for a customer, my view was and still is that O-I missed a golden opportunity to expand its product line using what was then our unique and proprietary plastic technology expertise and we again missed getting in on the ground floor of a brand new and permanent change in the evolving world of plastic packaging.

Oh well.

Perhaps the final "nail in the PET coffin" at O-I occurred in 1985 when, as Technical Director of O-I's Plastic Beverage Operations, I was one of several PBO executives who approached the O-I Board of Directors to ask for more capital to expand our very successful five-plant manufacturing operation.

However, when I looked down the table at the O-I Board made up primarily of former Glass Container executives including Chairman Ed Dodd and Corporate VP's Bill Spengler and Bob Lanigan, I could tell immediately that we were not going to get more money to expand a plastic container manufacturing business that was not only competing with O-I's glass container business but was actually winning, since more and more soft drink manufacturers were converting from glass and metal to plastic.

The O-I Board, of course, said no to our request for more capital which was pretty much the end of O-I's leadership position in the plastic PET bottle business. In fact, soon after that time, O-I sold the entire Plastic Beverage Operations business to Graham Packaging, but that is another story for another day.

47

O-I Business Card

O-I did reward me, however. I was promoted to become the Director of Plastics Technology and was made a Vice President for all O-I's plastics businesses, and I was also offered a nice office on the 23rd floor of the new O-I Headquarters Building in Downtown Toledo, looking out over the Maumee River.

But as I have preached to my children for years, "Life is never a straight line, so keep your eyes open and don't miss the unexpected opportunities when they come along."

Not long after that fateful board meeting, my unexpected opportunity came along when I was sitting in my grand office on the 23rd floor of the new O-I Building and looking out over the City of Toledo contemplating my new role as the director of O-I's 600 plastics technology employees, when the phone rang, and the call was from a Texas Coca-Cola bottler I had met along the way named John Dunagan.

John's question was simple. He said that if O-I was not going to expand the PET beverage bottle business, he was already embarking on the challenge of self-manufacturing his own bottles on site at his Coca-Cola bottling operation locations in Texas, and he asked whether I was interested in leaving O-I to help them make that happen.

In fact, John told me that several of his colleagues, including Dick Roswech, another friend of mine who had started up and run O-I's first PET bottle plant in Milford CT, had already begun the self-manufacturing business for Coca-Cola, but they wanted to expand that business and they wanted to develop other plastic PET packages such as a PET plastic can; and they needed technical expertise!

Industry Situation and Early PTI History

Since O-I was not planning to pursue the PET bottle business, I had no real conflict of interest when I left O-I. However, I did agree not to share competitive information, and I left O-I in December of 1985 to found Plastic Technologies, Inc. (actually, I first named my new enterprise Midwest Plastic Research Associates) with no bad feelings, and initially to help John Dunagan and Dick Roswech and the Coca-Cola Company leverage the concept of self-manufacturing their own plastic containers.

In fact, soon after founding PTI, O-I approached PTI to ask for our help in designing a novel rotary preform compression molding machine, which we did.

One trailer to the O-I Plastic Beverage Operations story, which I can only tell now that most of the former O-I glass executives will no longer read this story, is this. Three years after I had left O-I and founded PTI, I was asked to give a talk at the Rotary Club in downtown Toledo, which I did, and I used the opportunity to tell the story about the PET bottle.

As I was packing up my sample PET bottles in my brief case after the talk, I looked out into the audience and noticed the former O-I Chairman, Ed Dodd, who had obviously come to hear my speech.

As the room was clearing, Ed Dodd, who had retired from O-I by that time, walked up to the front of the room and looked up at me (I was on a stage) and just said "You know, Tom, we probably should have done that." And then, he walked away. That was the last time I ever saw Ed Dodd, and even today I hold no ill feelings.

I understood exactly why O-I made the decision that they did at the time, and had O-I decided to pursue PET, I would never have gotten the opportunity to start PTI and to pursue what has turned out to be an exciting and rewarding career as an entrepreneur.

One other little-known fact that reinforces why perhaps O-I should have pursued the PET bottle commercialization pathway is that when I was promoted to become the Plastics Technology Director, Paul Rothschild was then also promoted to become a VP in the O-I International Division, where he was tasked with licensing O-I technologies around the world. A little-known fact is that Paul was very successful at licensing O-I's PET technology in Chile, Venezuela, Australia, and elsewhere, and that those licensees were all very successful at commercializing O-I's PET technology and paid handsome royalties to O-I, at least until O-I abandoned the plastics packaging market altogether.

The Evolution of the PET Bottle Industry

The introduction of plastic was indeed the trigger that precipitated the move to self-manufacture in the soft drink industry because, heretofore, the options were only glass or metal, and the significant investment and centralized locations required for glass and metal container manufacturing operations do not lend themselves to distributed self-manufacture.

Plastic package manufacturing machinery, on the other hand, can be easily installed on site right next to the filling operations and offers total flexibility for manufacturing various sizes and types of containers.

Today, self-manufacture of plastic packaging is widespread, even beyond the beverage industry, and glass containers are only used today for more specialized packaging applications.

First Plastic Can

After I left O-I and began working to help Coca-Cola expand their plastic container manufacturing operations, and to develop a plastic can that would replace the metal can, I learned that John Dunagan and Coca-Cola had licensed the free-standing petaloid (footed) base technology from Continental PET Technologies and that they were working together with Continental and with Marty Beck in Amherst NH where the Continental R&D Labs were located.

Marty Beck

Of course, I did not yet have my own PTI laboratories during those first several years so my job was to work directly with Marty Beck and Continental to help expand the Coca-Cola self-manufacturing operations and to develop a 12 oz plastic can to replace the traditional metal can so that Coca-Cola could also consider self-manufacturing its own cans, just as they were doing with bottles.

Wayne and Kathleen Collette

During those first several years after leaving O-I, I got to know Marty Beck and his R&D team well because the Continental labs served as Coca-Cola's plastic labs and the Continental team, with me as the project manager, served as Coca-Cola's technical self-manufacture team. The CPET team included Wayne Collette, George Rollend, Tom Nahill, Suppayan Krishnakumar (the inventor of the petaloid base), Brad Molnar, Richard Clark, and Lou Tacito.

As the new Coca-Cola self-manufacture technical project manager, I had a chance to look inside the Continental laboratories and to meet the technical team that had been O-I's (my) number one competitor, because now this was my team to make things happen for Coca-Cola who had licensed the Continental PET technology.

To put it mildly, I was very impressed, because the Continental team had developed and patented the one-piece (no base cup required) PET bottle/can base designs and a new multilayer preform injection technology which are what Coca-Cola needed to self-manufacture their own PET bottles and to develop a multilayer/high barrier plastic 12 oz can.

Soon after the self-manufacture of beverage bottles happened, Continental, a world leader in the manufacture of metal beverage cans, apparently also began to question the compatibility of owning both plastic container and metal container manufacturing businesses since those internal businesses competed, as was the case at O-I with glass and plastic.

Continental Petaloid (footed) base

Further, John Dunagan and Coca-Cola began to recognize that the introduction of plastic PET beverage containers in large quantities would stimulate questions about the recyclability of the new plastic PET container. Metal cans and glass bottles were already recognized as being recyclable and in many parts of the country recycling was already underway.

However, PET plastic containers represented a new packaging medium for the beverage industry and John Dunagan and Dick Roswech and the Coca-Cola Company recognized early on that they had to address this question or risk a backlash against the introduction of a non-recyclable package at scale.

Perhaps coincidentally, the early consideration by Coca-Cola of how to promote the recyclability of PET and the nearly coincidental considerations by both O-I and Continental to divest of their investments in plastic led John Dunagan and his Coca-Cola self-manufacture colleagues to hire another project manager to address the question of PET recycling, as they had hired me to be the project manager for PET container self-manufacture.

Not surprisingly, they decided to approach Marty Beck at Continental to become the PET Recycling Project Manager, just as they had approached me to become the PET Manufacturing Technology Project Manager.

Just as I made my decision to leave O-I, in part, because O-I had become more concerned with the internal competition of plastic with glass, Marty I suspect, also made his decision to leave Continental because Continental was now becoming more concerned with the internal competition between plastic and metal.

In any case, the fact that both Marty and I happened to leave our respective Fortune 100 plastic packaging companies within a few months of each other and that we found ourselves teamed together to help Coca-Cola self-manufacture their own PET plastic bottles and to develop a viable national recycling strategy, turned into the opportunity of a lifetime for both of us.

Marty and I travelled together, we presented together, we studied together, we worked together, we gathered together with our families, and we certainly accomplished more together for Coca-Cola and for the PET industry because we joined forces during those early years.

Interestingly, even though Marty and I both established independent PET development companies and PET manufacturing companies and PET recycling companies, we never really competed with each other. In fact, we contracted overflow work out to each other when we couldn't handle all the work internally, because we respected and trusted one another.

Most importantly, however, we had the chance to really get to know one another, to work closely together in an industry that we had jointly helped create, and we were jointly successful at accomplishing the mission(s) that Coca-Cola and John Dunagan had in mind back in 1985.

"Ours is the one with the feet on it."

Marty passed way before his time at age 67 in 2019, but in 2018 as I was assembling my PET bottle history museum in my home shop (perhaps the only such museum in the world!), Marty and his wife, Jane, after his passing, shared with me several of his prized early PET and acrylonitrile bottle samples, and a very telling industry cartoon which I now have proudly displayed as part of my collection, and as a small tribute to a best friend.

The Early History of the PET Bottle Industry

Research and development relating to the use of PET (polyester) for commercial plastic bottle applications began in the late 1960's and intensified during the period 1971-1975. This R&D was carried out principally at several major plastics, glass, and can manufacturing companies in the US and in Europe who viewed the potential for PET bottles to replace both glass and cans as a threat to existing businesses and as an opportunity for new businesses.

As was discussed previously, two of the companies in the US which led this R&D effort included Continental Can Company (CCC), a leading package producer with a significant interest in protecting its aluminum can business, and Owens-Illinois, Inc. (O-I), also a leading package producer with a significant interest in protecting its glass bottle business.

Both CCC and O-I established substantial R&D efforts aimed at developing PET bottle technology and both companies led the commercialization of this technology for carbonated soft drink applications during the period from 1975-1982.

With the potential for high volume sales of PET plastic bottles to the soft drink industry (at that time combined sales of glass bottles and aluminum cans was approximately 50 billion containers), other companies also became interested in manufacturing PET bottles as well. While these companies, including Hoover Universal (then Johnson Controls, Inc., then Schmalbach Lubecca, and now AMCOR), Sewell Plastics (then Constar International, then Crown Cork & Seal and now CKS Packaging), Amoco Chemicals (now Silgan), and eventually PlastiPak Packaging, all established successful commercial businesses, none of these companies attempted to develop the fundamental technology bases that both CCC and O-I did during this period.

However, once the PET bottle business became commercial and successful, these new entrants into the manufacturing business quickly created an oversupply of containers and prices dropped dramatically. As prices fell and as supplies increased, it became apparent to the technical leaders, including CCC and O-I, that they would not only have difficulty in recouping their respective R&D investments, but that their respective can and glass bottle businesses were under severe attack from PET. Thus, both CCC and O-I eventually opted to sell their respective PET bottle businesses and to concentrate their commercial efforts on their more established and capital intensive can and glass bottle businesses.

Also, during the period from 1982-1985, the Coca-Cola bottlers in the Southwest and in the Southeast US became interested in manufacturing their own PET bottles rather than purchasing them from the established merchant suppliers, including all the companies named above, primarily because they could gain huge savings in their packaging costs. Regional Coca-Cola bottlers established four regional bottle making cooperatives, including Western Container Corp. (WCC) in the Southwest, Southeastern Container Inc. (SEC) in the Southeast, Apple Container Corp. (ACC) in New York, and FlorPak in Florida.

Behind WCC, SEC, and ACC was a man named John Dunagan who himself was a Coca-Cola bottler from Monahans, Texas, and a person who immediately saw the potential for all Coca-Cola bottlers to save millions of dollars by banding together and investing jointly in the self-manufacture of PET soft drink bottles. Marty Beck and I signed contracts with each of these Coca-Cola Coops and with the parent Coca-Cola Company to help them manufacture and recycle PET Bottles.

These regional PET self-manufacturing cooperatives became immensely successful within a matter of several years which put extreme pressure on the merchant manufacturers who had previously depended upon Coca-Cola and other soft drink manufacturers to purchase their PET bottles.

This stimulated the merchant suppliers like CCC and O-I to abandon the PET business completely, but other suppliers continued to focus on PET bottles by developing applications other than soft drink bottles in food, personal care, water, and other product categories, to replace the Coca-Cola self-manufacture business lost to these regional cooperatives.

The PET bottle manufacturers, machine manufacturers, and resin producers have therefore flourished since the early 1980's, and while Coca-Cola and several other personal care, water, and food brand owners have continued to nurture self-manufacture on a global basis, other brand owners have continued to purchase from merchant suppliers, and the "custom" PET bottle business for food, personal care, household chemical and other product applications has also grown dramatically.

At the same time, PET fiber, film, and engineered products applications have also continued to enjoy steady growth and today the PET resin, machine, and product manufacturing industries have become substantial factors in world commerce.

PET today is one of two dominant plastics used for plastic bottles, and PET has caused the demise of glass for many product applications including carbonated soft drinks (CSD), water, other beverages, food, household chemical, and personal care products.

Virtually all CSD, personal care, and household chemical packaging has already converted from glass to plastic due to factors such as low cost, safety, and environmental acceptability (recyclability).

While the PET resin and chemical industries service a wide spectrum of product applications, the PET bottle business has remained apart from other polyester manufacturing businesses since the technology for processing PET into bottles remains uniquely different from the technology for processing every other commodity plastic into a container shape. Thus, the numbers of people experienced in PET technology remains relatively low worldwide and the implementation and use of PET technology for bottle packaging applications remains a specialized field. Furthermore, since large companies have reduced their technical staffs substantially over the past twenty years, there has been limited opportunity for the development and training of experienced PET technologists, and the fact that the PET packaging industry continues to grow at such a rapid rate makes PET packaging technology development, implementation, and training a still valuable asset for companies engaged in the manufacture, sale, and use of PET containers.

Importance of the Coca-Cola Company

As an initial funding partner of PTI, along with the four Coca-Cola Cooperatives, Southeastern Container, Western Container, New York Coca-Cola (Apple Container), and Florida Coca-Cola (FlorPak), the Coca-Cola Company dedicated significant technical and financial resources to making the PET bottle and the Coca-Cola self-manufacture operations successful.

I hesitate to list all the Coca-Cola personnel who were essential to the success of the entire plastic beverage bottle industry because I will miss some of those names, but I must nevertheless mention several of those Coca-Cola technical and package development people who I worked closely with throughout the evolution of the industry and during those first 20 years, because they were also important to my success at both O-I and at PTI.

Dr. Forrest Bayer along with Scott Vitters led the corporate PET recycling efforts at Coca-Cola and Dr. Dan Dennison led the efforts to understand the impact of plastic packaging on product integrity. Mike Gage, Tim Exley, Mike Schultheis, Dan Denison, and Scott Summerville worked with suppliers like O-I and PTI to develop and qualify the many PET packages that evolved over those 20 years.

While the other soft drink companies also contributed to the evolution of the industry, it was my observation that Coca-Cola's early commitment to self-manufacture, to the development of a plastic can, and to their early commitment to developing a PET recycling strategy were keys to the evolution of the entire industry.

The Petainer PET Plastic Can Story

This story is courtesy of Mr. Peter Rose, retired Krupp-Corpoplast Technical Manager

PLM Group, the 1980's inventor of the first (commercial) plastic can and the process to manufacture that can, remains the largest Dassault Systèmes SolidWorks partner in Northern Europe, serving more than 5000 customers from a wide range of industries in Sweden, Denmark, Norway, Finland, Estonia and Latvia. In 1985 when PLM invented the Petainer plastic can and the solid-phase-pressure-forming process to make an oriented PET can, PLM asked Krupp Corpoplast to develop the commercial machinery and the control systems to manufacture the can.

The original development and approval process was completed on a 3-station LS-1 prototype production machine which was first installed at the PLM plant in Dongen Holland located close to the town of Tilburg. However, because PLM was not satisfied with the progress at Dongen, they requested a more experienced project manager from Corpoplast which is why Corpoplast general manager, Gunter Kleimenhagen, recommended that Peter Rose take over the project management for the experimental Petainer plastic can forming process.

In January of 1985 Peter Rose arrived at PLM in Dongen, and his first decision was to request an additional design team led by A. Appel that immediately began documenting the various mechanical issues and recommending improvements.

With local Tilburg machine tool providers available, Corpoplast quickly solved the major mechanical issue which was to optimize the design of the "stretch ring" that formed the oriented can from a PET process blank.

Once the team achieved a stable process, the metal stretch rings were hardened and polished and they also installed light-activated gates to control the final length of the stretched PET process blanks.

They also modified the dimensions of the heated mandrel so that the PET blanks were uniformly heated, and to assure a stable process they determined that no regrind could be used in the process.

Peter recalls that every Friday the team met to thoroughly review the week's progress and to share any modifications or process changes with every team member.

After just one month and by the beginning of February 1985 they were able to process quality cans which were quickly prepared for qualification.

During that first week in February 1985, they ran the pilot production machine 8 hours/day for 6 days and did maintenance on the 7th day.

Petainer was so satisfied with the improved processing of the PET Petainer cans that by March of 1985 Coca Cola and Constar were invited to visit and they approved a production trial.

During the period March to June 1985, they produced 150,000 Petainer plastic cans and delivered them to Coca-Cola in Atlanta for market testing in August of 1985.

The prototype cans were successfully filled by Coca-Cola in Columbus, Georgia in September of 1985, and according to Peter, not a single can was damaged during the filling process which took place on a conventional can filling line. By comparison, it was normal for the traditional thin-walled aluminium cans to occasionally fail during the filling process.

Barbara Rose, the Corpoplast Office Manager, visited the South Star Grocery in Columbus, Georgia in October 1985 to interview customers who had purchased and used the plastic cans, and she quickly learned that the new plastic can was highly accepted by the customers. Coca-Cola even used the slogan "Now Your Choice is Clear" to advertise the new plastic can.

PET Petainer plastic cans filled with Coca-Cola

PET Petainer plastic cans with the slogan," Now Your Choice is Clear!"

A Change in Plans

Peter Rose and chief designer, Peter Albrecht, spent most of 1986 improving the C-80 PET Petainer Machine since Coca-Cola had ordered 7 machines to be installed in Atlanta. Improvements involved everything from installing improved blank heating systems to automating the mechanical stretching mechanism to refining the tooling designs and by November 1986 the 7 machines were ready for shipment.

However, at the last minute Coca-Cola declined the shipment of the Corpoplast-Petainer machines, and to the surprise of both Petainer and Continental PET Technologies, Coca-Cola abandoned both the Petainer Plastic Can project and Continental PET Technologies' multilayer plastic can project during that same month in 1986, apparently because the aluminum can industry had suddenly realized that the plastic can was a legitimate competitor so had made an offer to Coca-Cola to sell them aluminum cans at a price that Coca-Cola "could not refuse."

This turn of events forced Petainer to quickly pursue a Plan B strategy which involved shipping the 4 Petainer plastic can machines to Atlanta but installing and operating those machines themselves while hoping to find another plastic can customer.

Indeed, Petainer successfully convinced New York Seltzer to qualify their seltzer products in the plastic can, and after the machines were installed in Atlanta, production quantities were shipped to New York Seltzer beginning in the summer of 1987.

After additional improvements to the machine, Petainer was able by the summer of 1988 to achieve running speeds of 12,000 cans/hour and efficiencies of 70% resulting in effective production rates of 8,400 cans/hour, a new record! However, by then it was also clear that the plastic can was just not going to find the commercial traction it required to support a high-volume plastic can production operation in the US.

Steps to produce a Petainer plastic can using a Solid Phase Pressure Forming Process

Solid Phase Pressure Forming Machine

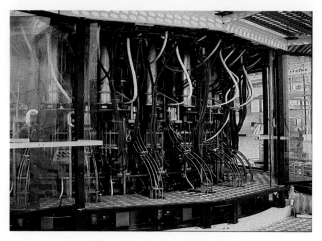

Solid Phase Pressure Forming Machine

Purchase of the entire Petainer Plant by Yamamura Glass Co.

In June 1988 Petainer Development arranged a visit to the Yamamura Group in Japan which included both Sewell Plastics and Krupp Corpoplast with the goal of moving the entire Petainer plastic can plant to Japan, since by then it was clear that the plastic can was not going to take off in the US.

After extensive meetings and negotiations between Yamamura, Petainer, and Krupp Corpoplast, an agreement was reached in August 1988 and the Petainer assets were acquired by Yamamura Glass Company Ltd.

By July 1989, all the Petainer machines had been shipped to Japan and were installed and operational. Yamamura was able to secure a contract with Canada Dry of Japan and began production of what was hoped to be the first sustainable Petainer plastic can application in the world.

Moving of the Petainer PET can technology from the US to Japan

Unfortunately, however, fate intervened once again when the Japanese government declared that beverages could not be packaged in PET containers smaller than 1.5 litres, presumably because of potential taste issues, not because of anything dangerous or toxic.

In November 1989 Yamamura and Petainer cancelled their contract, and even though the Petainer plastic can had performed well and was widely accepted by consumers, it found itself once again looking for a market.

Since the development of the Petainer plastic can technology, other suppliers have made attempts to develop a commercial plastic can, but the facts are that for small size containers, plastic does not offer the advantages in shelf life, safety, transparency, or cost that it does for large sized containers.

Coca-Cola's Influence on the PET Recycling Industry

This story is courtesy of Dr. Forrest Bayer, former Director of Recycling, and retired Coca-Cola Fellow

Much of the success of PET packaging can be attributed to the PET bottle design and performance breakthroughs achieved by Plastic Technologies, Inc., and Continental PET Technologies, but as PET packaging grew, the world began to realize that waste disposal and litter would become a real issue. The plastics industry had already begun developing effective recycling technologies for non-food contact plastics, but recycling PET for reuse back into food contact applications presented a new and more difficult challenge.

Johnson Controls, Inc. was the first company to obtain a letter of no objection (LNO) from the US FDA for direct food contact applications, but the US FDA stipulated that feedstock for the Johnson Controls process could only come from PET bottles collected from deposit states, meaning that no curbside-collected recycled PET could be used.

Dr. Forrest and Charlene Bayer

The Coca-Cola Company took the lead in addressing the question of using curbside-collected recycled PET by entering into a cooperative agreement with the Hoechst-Celanese Company in 1989 to investigate the use of chemical depolymerization via methanolysis as an approach to recycling PET back into food grade resin applications.

To their credit, Coca-Cola and Hoechst-Celanese were jointly successful in obtaining the first curbside Letter of No Objection (LNO) from the US FDA on January 9, 1990. Together they also initiated the first commercial trial using this technology in April of 1991, planning a commercial rollout of 25% recycled content PET Bottles (RPET) in September of that same year.

Coca-Cola continued to work with other PET producers to investigate other approaches to using RPET, including 1) the use of multi-layer packaging to keep the RPET from directly contacting the food product and 2) "super-cleaning" RPET using steam cleaning and high vacuum. But eventually, Coca-Cola and the industry came to realize that the cost and therefore the economics of chemical depolymerization would not be commercially sustainable.

Because there still are only 10 deposit states in the US, limiting the recycled PET supply to only deposit-grade RPET bottles was too restrictive, so The Coca-Cola Company approached PTI in 1996 to enter into a cooperative agreement to develop a proprietary approach that would allow the use of ALL postconsumer recycled PET back into food contact applications, including the use of curbside-collected RPET.

This ground-breaking development project code-named **CyclePET**™ was coordinated with PTI by Dr. Forrest Bayer of The Coca-Cola Company. In addition to his many other duties, Dr. Bayer became the key person to interface with the US FDA on the use of all recycled plastics in food contact applications.

Until that time, authorizations for direct food contact approaches through the US FDA's letter of no objection (LNO) process had been limited to 1) post-consumer plastics from deposit legislation states only, 2) curbside RPET which had been through chemical depolymerization, or 3) multilayer packaging where the RPET was not in direct food contact.

However, after rigorous "mechanical" recycling using Phoenix's proprietary **Small Particle Size Technology** proved successful, Dr. Bayer and Phoenix Technologies shared data with the US FDA demonstrating that either 100% deposit or 100% curbside-collected post-consumer RPET could be recycled to achieve the degree of purification required by the US FDA. This data was used to apply for an LNO from the US FDA and approval for use of The **Phoenix Process**™ (US Patent #20070246159-A1 to Donald W. Hayward and Daniel L. Witham) was granted to Phoenix Technologies in August of 1999 and became the first post-consumer PET mechanical recycling technology approved to use either post-consumer deposit or post-consumer curbside PET to produce new direct food contact packages.

This was a critically important achievement because there was a huge cost differential between deposit grade and curbside recycled PET. The use of curbside material made recycling PET economical. The Coca-Cola Company was so enthusiastic about the potential for the new **Phoenix Process**™ that it wanted to quickly expand the use of food contact-approved recycled PET into other countries.

The priority country for the Coca-Cola Company was Australia, so Dr. Bayer worked with the Australian regulatory authorities and obtained authorization for the **Phoenix Process**™ to be used in Australia. After obtaining the necessary approvals, the recycling plant built in Preston, Australia just north of Sydney and close to Coca-Cola Amatil Ltd. became the first commercial operation in Australia to use post-consumer deposit or curbside RPET in direct food contact packaging.

Coca-Cola Amatil Ltd then licensed the PTI/Phoenix PET recycling technology to begin the internationalization of the PET recycling industry, and the Coca-Cola Company and the industry moved from using PET as a third soft drink packaging option to making PET the primary option.

The Development of the PepsiCo PET Returnable Bottle

This story is courtesy of Mr. Mark Niemiec, former Director of Packaging for PepsiCo-Cola International

Mark Niemiec

During a discussion with Tom Brady, I mentioned the story behind the development of PepsiCo PET Returnable bottle. Tom asked me to add a chapter to this book. My name is Mark Niemiec, and I was the Director of Packaging for PepsiCo International from 1985 to 1989.

I joined the PepsiCo International (PCI) Division after two years in the PepsiCo USA Division fighting the "Cola Wars." I left after putting space cans on the Challenger and after successfully growing PepsiCo's market share in both single serve and multipack PET bottles and aluminum cans. I was even given a day off when the "other guy blinked" (meaning when Coca-Cola made the mistake of launching "New Coca-Cola" which never gained market acceptance). However, perhaps the most significant industry dynamic during those early days was the launch of the 2-liter PET bottle in 1978, which changed the entire competitive infrastructure in the US soft drink bottling business.

To provide a little history, when I took over the PCI Packaging role, it was clear that Bob Beebe, then the Division President, wanted to have a plastic returnable bottle in his arsenal to serve the international markets that were already dependent on returnable glass bottles.

Supporting Mr. Beebe's strategic direction, the European country leading the soft drink market growth at the time was Germany where the introduction of disposable PET bottles was not popular and where the established beverage industry had been historically committed to returnable glass and was successfully encouraging the German government to resist one-way plastic packaging.

Not surprisingly, therefore, it was rumored that Coca-Cola was developing a plastic returnable bottle for the German market.

When I arrived, PCI was exploring the development of a returnable bottle for the European market using Monsanto's acrylonitrile resin, but when I and PCI learned that Coca-Cola was developing a PET returnable bottle for the German market, we quickly changed PCI's focus and redirected our resources toward helping PCI to catch up with Coca-Cola by also developing a returnable bottle for the European market.

Fortunately, I had Chris Mero on staff, and I also had a consulting contract with Jack Cahill who had a long history with PepsiCo and was on the initial PepsiCo team that work with DuPont to develop the PET bottle technology. Chris had worked with me in PepsiCo USA and was very instrumental in the early expansion of PET in the US market, so he also had a solid PET bottle technology background.

Our first effort to reach for outside technical resources was to approach Tom Brady at PTI. Unfortunately, however, PTI could not work with PepsiCo since they were already committed to Coca-Cola.

So, after a couple of false starts with different US PET suppliers, PCI focused on partnering with a regional PET supplier in Holland which was consistent with PCI's initial target market.

As it turned out, PCI's bottler in Holland (Europe) was Heineken and they wanted a PET returnable bottle, so it was a perfect fit to have the local PET supplier in Holland become our partner.

The development of a returnable PET bottle presented several major technical challenges:

- First, to be economically viable the bottle had to survive at least 15+ refill cycles. This meant that the bottle had to be designed with bottle-to-bottle touch points that would minimize sidewall abrasion and the sidewalls had to be strong enough to handle the rigors of distribution and a refillable system.
- The bottle also had to be safe after reuse, meaning there could be no residual contaminants. Since there is no way to know what was put in a bottle by the consumer before it is returned for refilling, which was not an issue with glass which is inert, a plastic refillable bottle represented a new and unproven challenge.
- A new contaminant detector had to be invented to sample every bottle prior to washing. This detector became known as the "sniffer" because a probe was inserted into the bottle to sample the headspace and to detect whether a non-safe chemical had been stored in the bottle by the consumer.
- The bottle also had to withstand the rigors of a glass refillable bottle washing system which employed high temperatures and used caustic cleaning chemicals. As it turned out, PET could not handle the abuse in the existing glass bottle refillable cleaning system, so lower temperature cleaning products had to be identified.
- Finally, it was important that the bottle design properly reflect the all-important PepsiCo brand image.

The above challenges required the development of much more sophisticated high-tech cleaning technologies as well as new ways of operating a returnable system if the industry was to introduce a viable and sustainable commercial product.

Each challenge turned out to be a separate project for the PCI technology team. The engineering group, for example, had to identify an equipment manufacturer that could modify an existing piece of equipment to create the sniffing machine. A prominent filling equipment manufacturer that offered a rotary mechanical base was eventually selected. The engineering group also had to contract a high-tech company to design and produce the sniffing probe technology along with the control electronics that were to be installed on the modified filling machine. Reliability was critical because it was important to assure the safety and integrity of the beverage in every one of the refilled bottles.

To better understand the safety exposure of contaminated bottles, PCI contracted with Battelle to conduct a broad study of chemicals that could be absorbed by the PET. That study eventually provided the data needed by the sniffer equipment team to design a headspace sampling profile which would detect and discard any bottle with a safety concern.

The design of the PET returnable bottle broke new ground for PET beverage containers and it became clear that the selection of the right grade of PET resin and the design of the preform were both critical. Since PCI's target market was Holland and not Germany, it was necessary to carry out a serious industrial intelligence effort in the PET container manufacturing space so that PCI's suppliers could gain the necessary insights to accelerate the development of the PCI bottle and to keep pace with Coca-Cola's launch plans for Germany.

PepsiCo-Cola's Returnable/Refillable Plastic PET Bottle - 1989

The race to develop a returnable plastic PET bottle was a unique example of the intensity of the **"Cola Wars"** that took place in the 1980's.

We were all pleased when, after several filling trials, several simulation tests, and a few million dollars, we finally had a viable commercial PET returnable bottle. The launch of the Pepsi-Cola 1.5-Liter PET returnable bottle took place in early 1989 and within months of Coca-Cola's launch of their PET returnable bottle in Germany. As I look back on my role in packaging, the development of PepsiCo's first PET returnable bottle was perhaps the most significant technical challenge of my entire career which, I am pleased to say, resulted in being awarded the PCI Technical Leadership Award in 1989!

The Story of Husky Injection Molding Systems

Taken, in part, from the 2005 Master's thesis of Newton Kewl
(https://www.writework.com/essay/husky-injection-molding-systems

Robert Schad emigrated to Canada from Germany in 1951 and founded Husky in 1953. As an engineer by training, Schad started Husky to design and manufacture snowmobiles, but his first model, the "Huskymobile," was a complete failure.

To salvage his business, he quickly turned to machining jobs for other customers which eventually led him into the business of machining injection molds.

He was only able to compete by underbidding the competition and losing money on his first few jobs, but his strategy turned out to be a sound strategy because by the late 1950's Husky became recognized as a high-quality manufacturer of plastic injection molds.

In 1961, Mr. Schad and Husky created their first plastic injection molding machine for thin wall products but when sales did not materialize, Husky was forced to declare bankruptcy. However, Mr. Schad stuck with the mission of supplying both molds and machines and by the mid 1960's, customers began to purchase Husky equipment because they liked the fully integrated machine/mold approach.

However, the oil embargo in the early 1970's which caused the price of plastics to soar, again put Husky on the verge of bankruptcy. This time Husky was saved by Owens-Illinois. Husky needed a qualified injection PET mold/machine buyer as a partner and O-I became that partner by providing Husky with proprietary PET injection mold modeling technology, in exchange for Husky guaranteeing O-I exclusive use of Husky PET machinery and molds.

Mr. Schad did not have much choice in 1973 so Husky and O-I signed an agreement which worked out very well for both Husky and O-I.

Although Husky was an early exclusive supplier to O-I, by the late 1970's and when Husky was again solvent, O-I and Husky renegotiated their agreement which gave Husky the right to sell molds and machines to the industry while O-I retained the right to have only O-I's molds designed with O-I's proprietary hot runner designs.

To his great credit, Robert Schad took Husky from the brink of bankruptcy in the early 1970s to become the leading PET injection mold and machine supplier in the world by 1995, with an estimated 60% of the world market.

Profits from the sale of PET molds and machines provided the runway that Husky needed to expand during the 1980s and 1990s into other materials and product applications. Today, Husky remains a leading industry supplier.

Husky's sales exploded from $250M in 1992 to nearly $600M by 1995 and return on equity approached 40%, an unheard-of level for the plastics processing machine supply industry.

However, also by 1995, many quality competitors around the world emerged and prices for molds and machine came under intense pressure.

By January of 1996, Mr. Schad and his management team decided to eliminate the production of the more cost competitive closure (plastic caps) mold business and to concentrate again on PET machines and molds.

In 1998, PET remained the fastest growing plastic injection molding material market and PET bottles were now wanted, not just for soft drinks, but also for the water, beverage, food, and even the beer markets, so the Husky strategy was timely.

In 2022, Husky still manufactures a wide range of injection molding machines, molds, hot runners, robots, and auxiliary systems that are used in plastics manufacturing.

Husky's head office and primary manufacturing site remain in Bolton, Ontario, Canada, and Husky also has manufacturing facilities in the United States, Czechia, Luxembourg, Brazil, China, and India. Sales, parts, and technical support centers are also located across the globe.

Husky still specializes in PET for beverage packaging products and still controls more than 50% of the global market for PET processing systems.

What has changed for Husky is ownership. Husky Injection Molding Systems Ltd. was a publicly traded company from 1998 to 2007, although Robert Schad was still the controlling shareholder with 44% of the stock. The company's common shares were listed on the Toronto Stock Exchange.

However, on December 13, 2007, the Canadian private equity investment firm Onex completed a friendly buyout of Husky for C$960 million.

On November 17, 2009, Onex announced that it planned to sell its stake in Husky in a new initial public offering though it did not sell during that time of recession.

On December 17, 2010, however, it was reported that Onex had started talks to sell Husky to rival buyout firms intending to fetch C$2 billion.

Berkshire Partners LLC, the Boston-based private equity firm, and OMERS Private Equity Inc., the private equity arm of the OMERS Worldwide group of companies, announced the successful closing of their previously announced acquisition of Husky International Ltd on June 30, 2011.

And finally, on December 18, 2017, it was announced that Platinum Equity agreed to acquire Husky Injection Molding Systems from Berkshire Partners and OMERS Private Equity for $3.85 billion.

Robert Schad no longer has any ownership in the Husky company that he founded in 1953 but he went on to found another injection molding machine company, Athena, in 2013 and remains active in the industry.

History of Group Sidel S.A.

Story and photos from:

Wikipedia https://en.wikipedia.org/wiki/Sidel,

Encyclopedia.com https://www.encyclopedia.com/books/politics-and-business-magazines/groupe-idel-sa

Reference for Business https://www.referenceforbusiness.com/history2/81/Groupe-Sidel-S-A.html#ixzz7AcLPnaq3

March, 2020 Petnology Magazine - Interview with Vincent LeGuen, Sidel Vice President of Packaging and former General Manager of PTI-Europe, and Monica Brim, Sidel CEO https://www.petnology.com/competence-magazine/news-details/how-does-sidel-view-the-issue-around-pet.html

"The Sidel Saga1961-1998," a Sidel Group History Published by The Sidel Group in 1997

Monica Grim, Sidel CEO, 2019

Vincent LeGuen, Sidel VP Packaging, 2015

Jean-Pierre Lanctuit, Sidel International Sales, 1978

Francis Olivier, Sidel CEO, 1972

The Sidel Group began with Paul Lesieur's 1961 agreement with inventor, Antoine Di Settembrini in Le Havre, France, to design and build machines to make polystyrene bottles for jars of cream and yogurt.

From that very first blow molding machine design effort, Group Sidel has evolved to become a global plastic blow molding machine builder that has continually developed new packaging technologies for the food, beverage, and personal care industries.

As early as 1961 Lesieur's company developed the first plastic polyvinyl chloride (PVC) bottle for edible oil and subsequently for wine, milk, and water, and in 1973 Sidel created the first stretch-blow molded plastic HDPE (high density polyethylene) bottle for milk which was sterilized using Sidel's patented Ultra-Heat Treatment (UHT) technology

In 1980, under the leadership of Francis Olivier who had arrived as CEO in 1972 and with the sales tenacity of Jean-Pierre Lanctuit, Sidel delivered its first PET blow molding machine to the family-owned soft-drink company, Barraclough, in Great Britain and Sidel and Jean-Pierre subsequently established machine sales in several countries, including the US, where even though he could not sell to Owens-Illinois because of O-I's exclusive agreement with Corpopplast, Jean-Pierre was able to sell a machine to Marty Ryan at Amoco Containers.

In 1981, Jean-Pierre attended the Ryder (PET) Conference in Cherry Hill, NJ where he first met Dave Cook and Ken Halsall from Husky Injection Molding Systems in Canada, which was the beginning of a long and successful collaboration between Sidel that made PET stretch-orientation blow molding machines and Husky that was the leader in manufacturing PET preform machines to produce the PET preforms that fed the Sidel blow molding machines.

By 1984, Jean-Pierre and Sidel convinced Marty Ryan to move to Atlanta, Georgia and to establish Sidel's first international machinery sales subsidiary, since the US was clearly where the PET blow molding machine market was going to grow quickly.

Francis Olivier

Sidel Super Combi   *Sidel Actis Matrix Combi*

During the 1990s Sidel acquired the French companies Hema (1995), Cermex (1996), and Gebo (1997), and in 1997 Sidel introduced a system which combined blow molding, filling, and capping.

In the same year, the first Sidel preform decontamination system using H_2O_2 spray was launched with Combi Disis.

The development of an internal carbon-based coating system in 1999 improved the barrier properties of PET packages to gases (O2 and CO2) which qualified PET bottles for beer applications,

In 2003, Sidel joined Tetra Laval and in 2005 Sidel merged with the Italian company, Simonazzi. Simonazzi was founded in 1850 with headquarters in Parma, Italy.

In 2006 Sidel launched Predis™, its dry decontamination solution technology for preforms and in April 2013 Sidel announced the launch of a new company as part of the Sidel Group, Gebo Cermex. Gebo Cermex focuses on engineering, line integration, and end-of-line packaging.

Today, Groupe Sidel S.A. is the world's leading designer, manufacturer, and distributor of machinery for PET (polyethylene terephthalate) bottling and packaging. Sidel's line of PET packaging machines, which range in speeds from 500 to 50,000 bottles per hour, have captured 60% of the world market for PET packaging, including 80% of the US market and more than 90% of the company's home market, France. Sales of Sidel's PET machines account for most of the company's total sales, but the company has maintained a presence in the PVC (polyvinyl chloride) and high-density polyethylene (HDPE) bottling and packaging equipment markets.

During the mid-1990s Sidel grew through acquisitions and entered other packaging machinery markets, including the manufacture and sale of shrink-wrapping and corrugated cardboard machines.

With subsidiaries in Spain, Italy, Brazil, the United States, Hong Kong, Malaysia, Singapore, Mexico, Germany, and the United Kingdom, Sidel has sold more than 1,400 PET blow molding machines in more than 90 countries which range in price up to US $5 million per machine.

Today, exports represent more than 90% of Sidel's sales, with its largest markets in Europe (41%) and North America (21%). The Far East is also fast becoming a principal market for PET bottling and packaging machinery and provides 20% of Sidel's total sales. A slump in the U.S. PET market led to a drop in Sidel's 1996 sales, down to Fr 3.12 billion, from the previous year's Fr 3.7 billion.

Sidel was led for many years by president-director-general Francis Olivier who together with other members of management, owned some 11% of Sidel's stock.

An interesting company history

Until the late 1950s, liquid consumer products such as soft drinks, mineral water, and others, were packaged almost exclusively in reusable glass bottles. Yet, glass bottles were expensive both for the producer and the consumer, prone to breakage, and heavy to transport. Manufacturers began seeking new, disposable packaging materials, and in the United States packagers turned to metal, cardboard, and plastics. These new packaging trends soon caught the attention of European producers, and among the first of the Europeans to seek alternatives to glass bottling was France's Lesieur, the leading European distributor of vegetable oils.

In 1961, that company's chairman, Paul Lesieur, met with inventor Antoine Di Settembrini who had developed a machine for producing polystyrene containers for yogurt, cream, and other products, and Lesieur recruited Di Settembrini to develop new packaging machinery for Lesieur's oils. In July 1961, Di Settembrini was given the responsibility for a new Light Packaging division based in the port of Le Havre, France.

Di Settembrini's attention turned quickly from polystyrene to a new form of plastic being developed at the time, polyvinyl chloride (PVC). PVC showed great promise with its light weight, strength, and ability to be molded into a variety of forms, and while food-grade PVC had yet to be developed, Di Settembrini and the Light packaging division set to work designing machinery to convert PVC into containers for Lesieur's products. By the end of 1961 the division had spent nearly a billion French francs to develop the necessary equipment and machine tools.

The division even began developing its own food-grade PVC compound and started production of its first bottles in October 1962. That attempt proved somewhat of a disaster, as the bottles shattered during the season's first frost. Meanwhile, the division was having more success in creating its machines and after just 18 months of preparation the division debuted its first bottle-making machine, dubbed the DSL-3 (named after Di Settembrini and Lesieur). The machine could produce 1,500 to 1,800 bottles per hour and by 1963 the division was ready to supply Lesieur with its first plastic bottles. Meanwhile, the division established its own research branch and formed a joint-venture partnership, Doryl, with the French chemical products arm of Shell to develop new plastic packaging materials.

The Lesieur machine and the plastic bottles it produced quickly caught the attention of other liquid container producers as well as the producers of liquids, notably the French wine industry. Liquids in the bottles proved to keep as well or better than in glass bottles, and at the same time, the plastic bottles weighed substantially less than their glass counterparts, proving much less expensive to transport. Lesieur briefly looked at licensing its technology, selling licenses to Italy's Massighisolfi (later AFE) and to Japan's Sumitomo.

However, Lesieur quickly changed course and determined instead to manufacture and to sell the machines its Light Packaging division had designed, and by the end of 1963 the division's newly formed commercial sales unit had had sold 14 of the DSL-3 machines. The following year sales rose to 20 machines, and in 1965 the company sold a total of 24 machines, including 3 of the new the DSL-2 model machines. Purchase price of the DSL machines was Fr 500,000. The division's revenues reflected the growing interest in its machines, increasing from Fr 6 million in 1963 to Fr 15 million in 1965 and with exports already accounting for 39 percent of revenues.

The future appeared to be bright for the division, especially with the interest of Vittel, one of the leading French producers of mineral water that had begun purchasing bottle-making machinery. That business opportunity, however, was temporarily put on hold when the French government decided to evaluate the approval for using plastic bottles for mineral water. The delay in approval and a slump in machinery sales in the mid-1960s put a brake on the division's growth, and the division was forced to reduce its work force which had grown from a team of 30 in 1961 to more than 300 by 1964. Nevertheless, the division had already grown out of its 'startup' phase and was moving into a new era as an industrialized company.

In 1965, the division was incorporated as an independent company, although remaining under the control of Lesieur. That new company was named Sidel, which stood for Société Industrielle des Emballages Légers. Sidel was 90 percent owned by Lesieur, while 10 percent was held by Pont-à-Mousson S.A., a subsidiary of French industrial giant Saint Gobain. Later that year, Sidel received another boost when COPLAIT, a Paris-based milk cooperative, purchased two DSL-3 machines for its pasteurized milk. Other milk producers soon followed, including such leading companies as Bridel, Totalpac, and Unicolait.

By then, Sidel's PVC packaging technology was the most advanced in the world. The company's DSL line was expanding with the DSL-3 reaching speeds of 3,000 units per hour, and Sidel also offered the high-speed DSL-4 and the smaller capacity DSL-1. The DSL-3 continued to be the company's flagship, however, and by the end of the decade more than 150 DSL-3s were in operation around the world.

In 1968, Sidel received a new lift when the French government finally approved the use of PVC for bottling mineral water.

However, the last half of the 1960s were difficult years for Sidel since Di Settembrini left the company, which led to years of litigation that would not be resolved until the beginning of the next decade. In the meantime, Sidel over-anticipated the growth of its sales and began hiring new employees, building a total work force of 417 people. Yet sales remained relatively modest, reaching only some Fr 45 million by the end of the decade. At the same time, the company's research and development efforts were floundering, and several of the company's machines, including the DSL-4, proved to be flawed. In disarray, Sidel reorganized its management and operations and began a new expansion program.

The "Black Years" 1973--86

Sidel's expansion plans failed, however, and by 1971 Sidel's sales had slipped back to Fr 40 million. The following year, Pont-à-Mousson S.A. took 100 percent control of Sidel, and the company entered what it would later refer to as its "black years." Sidel was attached to its new parent's mechanical division as the equipment and packaging division.

Sidel initially appeared to benefit from its new status. Its manufacturing operations were improved, allowing its production lines to develop from the somewhat makeshift quality of its early years to a truly industrialized unit. Pont-à-Mousson also invested heavily in building up the division's research and development activities, allowing Sidel to regain its reputation for innovation.

In 1973, the division debuted its DSL-3500, capable of producing 3,600 polyethylene bottles per hour. In that same year, Sidel introduced another new machine, the SAP-100, suited for producing small polyethylene aerosol spray containers for the perfume industry. The SAP-100 became one of the company's biggest successes during the 1970s.

However, Pont-à-Mousson's plans to expand its industrial division cast a shadow over Sidel's operations. In 1972, the parent had purchased Kaufman, a maker of industrial extruders. In 1974, Pont-à-Mousson added another acquisition, Billion, a maker of injection presses. In that same year, the three companies were joined together with Pont-à-Mousson's own industrial plants and formed into a new machinery division. At the end of 1974, the operations of Sidel, Kaufman, and Billion were formally merged into a new subsidiary, Société des Machines Pour la Transformation des Plastiques (SMTP) and the new company was headquartered in Nancy.

Merging the different organizational structures and operations of the three companies was a difficult task. At the same time, the parent company insisted that SMTP buy its parts from Pont-à-Mousson's own factories, which resulted in cost increases of as much as one-third. Sidel continued to produce new packaging machinery, including the first machine capable of producing PVC bottles for the important carbonated beverage market. For much of the 1970s, however, Sidel's activities were largely eclipsed by the attention paid to SMTP's Kaufman and Billion operations. Nevertheless, by the early 1980s, Sidel-- which had been developing its SBO series, capable of producing some 15,000 bottles per hour, became the dominant operation of the SMTP trio.

In 1984, after suffering losses totaling some Fr 72 million since the SMTP merger, Kaufman was sold to EMS; SMTP itself was restructured as Groupe Sidel, but two years later Sidel found itself again under threat. Pont-à-Mousson announced its intention to sell the Sidel operations to the German company, Krupp, and to Krupp's subsidiary, Corpoplast, a PET blow molding machine company that had long been Sidel's principal rival in the packaging machinery market.

The sale would have meant not only the passing of the French company into German hands, but it most likely would have meant the end of Sidel's activities altogether. Appealing to ultimate parent Saint Gobain, itself owned by the French government, Sidel's management, led by Francis Olivier, gained an agreement to perform a management buyout. Olivier put together a group of investors, including Jean-Pierre Lanctuit, who paid Saint Gobain Fr 108 million to purchase Sidel. Olivier and Jean-Pierre Lanctuit then led Sidel into its next phase, one of explosive growth.

The PET Conversion of the 1980s

By then, environmental pressures had long been threatening the use of PVC for product packaging and in the mid-1970s, producers in the United States had begun experimenting with a new form of plastic called polyethylene terephthalate, or PET, which would come to rival, and ultimately to surpass, PVC as the packaging material of choice, particularly for carbonated beverages.

Sidel's association with PET came rather late, but in 1977, Sidel entered into an agreement to share technology with Belgium's Solvay & Cie S.A., which led to the development of the company's BO (bi-orientation) PVC-based machines. At the same time, however, through its partnership with Solvay, Sidel decided to enter the PET market as well and Sidel's work on its first PET machine continued through the end of the decade.

The company initially approached mineral water company Vichy to produce PET machines for that company's carbonated water. Vichy, however, under pressure from the glass industry, balked. Instead, Sidel's first order came from Britain's Barraclough, a family-owned soft drink maker. Sidel delivered its first PET machine, the SBO-10, which was capable of processing 3,600 bottles per hour, in September 1980.

Sidel's next step was to bring its machines to the United States, by far the world's largest market for carbonated beverages. The American market held little interest for the French company's machines, but in 1980, the company attracted the interest of Amoco Container. The two companies reached an agreement, under which Amoco agreed to purchase Sidel machines, while Sidel agreed to increase the speed of its SBO (In French – Soufflage Bi-Orienté – meaning Bi-oriented blowing) series.

In 1981, Sidel debuted the SBO-24, capable of producing an industry-leading 15,000 blow-molded 16-ounce PET bottles per hour. Amoco, however, judging that the U.S. market was not ready for the half-liter bottle (indeed, that market did not yet even exist) backed out of its agreement with Sidel.

Sidel's PVC machines continued to make up the bulk of its sales for the first half of the 1980s and the sale of the SBO series remained minimal. However, in 1983, the company seized on a new sales tactic; it offered the SBO-24 free for six months and told customers that only if the machine worked, would the client have to pay.

This was a bold sales strategy, but a South Carolina-based bottler for PepsiCo was the first to take up the company's offer and bought the machine at the end of its six months. Next, Coca Cola bought its first SBO-24 in 1984, finally opening the U.S. market for Sidel's machines and the 16-ounce format. When Coca Cola decided to introduce a new three-liter bottle, it discovered that the only machine capable of producing these large bottles at high-speeds was Sidel's SBO-24.

From consolidated sales of Fr 85 million in 1979 based almost entirely on the company's PVC machines, Sidel's revenues grew to Fr 337 million in 1986, with its SBO series of PET machines accounting for one-third of its sales. That percentage would shift even more dramatically after the company achieved its independence in the mid-1980s, and Sidel's sales more than tripled by the end of the decade. The PET era was firmly underway.

Between 1977 and 1990, the industry grew from annual production of 10,000 tons of PET bottles to nearly one billion tons and Sidel eclipsed Corpoplast and the other PET blow molding machine manufacturers because Sidel was positioned at the forefront of the market's technology, quickly achieving worldwide market dominance as well.

By the beginning of the 1990s, the company's machines were present in 26 countries, including Eastern Europe, the Far East, and South America.

Leading the PET Market in the 1990s

Sidel's sales passed the Fr 1 billion in 1991 and the company continued to build on its successes, increasing the speed of the SBO-24 to 30,000 bottles per hour, while extending the SBO range to include the SBO-4, SBO-10, and the SBO-16 models, which offered diversity in both speed and bottle capacity. The company also introduced its very high-speed unit, the SBO-40, which boasted speeds of some 40,000 bottles per hour, four times faster than its nearest competitor.

By the mid-1990s, Sidel had passed the 50,000-bottle-per-hour mark with the introduction of the SBO 48/38. Sidel's marketing approach helped its machines expand beyond the initial soft-drink market, and instead of simply selling machines, Sidel's sales force concentrated on introducing new types of packaging in PET. By the mid-1990s, Sidel's PET machines were supplying a diverse range of some 30 product applications and Sidel PET blow molders were also driving the company's growth. By 1995, more than 86 percent of Sidel's sales were SBO series machines and the booming demand for the more environmentally friendly PET packaging helped Sidel's revenues triple again, to Fr 3.7 billion.

After achieving worldwide dominance in the PET market, Sidel expanded its focus and, in the mid-1990s, the company decided to diversify its operations, entering many new packaging markets.

During this period of rapid growth, Sidel began a series of acquisitions, adding the purchases Ouest Conditionnement (shrink-wrapping machines), Héma Technologies, Rémy, and Kalix (container filling machines), and Cermex (corrugated case packing and pelletizing machines). At the same time, Sidel began eyeing one of the most important markets of all, the beer market. With a goal of transitioning the beer market to PET bottles, in 1997 Sidel acquired the operations of Gebo Industries, a leading packaging for beer and soft drink products.

Looking to the future, Sidel envisioned even further expansion since by the mid 1990's PET still accounted for less than one-third of the soft drink and mineral water markets, only 4 percent of the fruit juice market, and a negligible portion of the alcoholic beverage market. Even today, Sidel continues as one of the leading PET blow molding machine suppliers in the world.

The Story of Plastic Technologies, Inc.

Thomas E Brady, PhD

I founded PTI in 1985 because I had an unusual background as the former VP and Director of Plastics Technology for Owens-Illinois, Inc. and because, even as a young plastics research engineer, I had been assigned responsibility for leading the technical and commercial development of PET bottle technology at O-I during the period 1971-1984.

The premise for creating PTI was that the Coca-Cola bottlers who had embarked on a successful PET bottle self-manufacturing course during the period 1981-1984 were seeking to expand their efforts and to undertake the development of new and innovative PET plastic soft drink packaging products, including for example, a PET plastic can. To accomplish these goals, the four Coca-Cola self-manufacturing cooperatives agreed to jointly sponsor and fund several major product development and engineering projects, and they set about to hire an experienced individual to manage these projects for the combined cooperatives.

Well known to many bottlers and managers in the Coca-Cola self-manufacture system because of my previous history and experience in PET technology and in the soft drink industry, I was approached by the Coca-Cola self-manufacture cooperatives about the opportunity to leave O-I and to manage these project development efforts for the Coca-Cola System.

Initially I declined the offer, even though it was an exciting opportunity because, as I recall, I didn't want to just change employers, but when I decided to make a counter proposal to the Coca-Cola cooperatives to establish a separate independent company for the purpose of managing these projects, the Coca-Cola Cooperatives agreed.

I was then able to create a new company, Plastic Technologies, Inc., with me as the only employee, and I was able to negotiate long-term contractual agreements with the four Coca-Cola Cooperatives and with the Coca-Cola Company.

The contracts assured PTI of initial funding, required me to manage the Plastic Can development project, and for PTI to carry out other engineering and technical development projects for the combined Coca-Cola Cooperatives, at their direction.

1987 The Founding PTI Management Team
Albert Uhlig, Betsy Brady, Scott Steele, Tom Brady,
Bob Deardurff, Marilee Spann, Frank Semersky

1995 PTI Senior Management Team
Scott Steele, Frank Schloss, Donald Miller, Donald Hayward,
Dan Durham, Tom Carros, Betsy Brady, Tom Brady, Tracy
Momany, Frank Semersky, Bob Deardurff

The contractual funding also provided sufficient credibility for our new enterprise to quickly identify additional customers who did not compete with Coca-Cola, and to attract and hire an experienced professional staff to carry out the technical development projects for the Coca-Cola Cooperatives and for those other early PTI customers.

While every one of those early "intrapreneurs" who helped me to create PTI and the PTI subsidiary companies that followed was important to our success, perhaps the most important of those early colleagues was my wife and best friend and mother to our 3 children and grandmother to our now 12 grandchildren, Betsy Brady.

I and my plastic technology colleagues were very good at providing technical development and manufacturing services to our many customers, but none of us had the capability to organize and manage the administrative side of the business, including hiring and organizing our human resource, finance, and administrative services activities, and becoming what I like to call "the soul of our business."

Tom and Betsy Brady

After 35 years, most of us who started and ran the technical side of the business are retired, but with second generation management throughout the PTI organization, Betsy is still there providing the continuity to the next generation of PTI's businesses. Perhaps as importantly, it was Betsy who encouraged me to leave a secure VP's job at a Fortune 100 company with 3 young children still at home and with essentially no business experience, and to take advantage of what turned out to be a once-in-a-lifetime opportunity. Had she told me that it was too risky and that I had better focus on having a secure job and raising our kids, I would not have made the leap. So, thanks, Betsy!

As PTI became immersed in important development programs for several other customers, and as PTI quickly established a reputation in the industry as a high-quality PET R&D and technical support resource, we expanded our technical staff to service those customers.

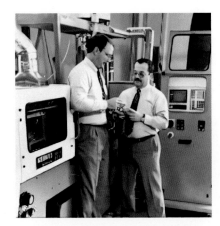

Bob Deardurff & Frank Semersky

Tracy Momany & Dan Durham

Frank Semersky & Keith Brown

Frank Schloss & Scott Steele

Dan Durham & Keith Brown

Gary Landis & Frank Schloss

2000 PTI Company Picture

As PTI's technical staff expanded and as the revenue base grew at compound annual rates of 35%, the company moved in 1994 from its rented office facility in downtown Toledo to a larger development facility in the suburb of Holland, Ohio where we upgraded our analytical testing and processing laboratories and expanded our PET container and preform prototyping capabilities.

PTI Headquarters at Wolf Creek Executive Park 1994-1997

During this period of rapid growth and expansion, PTI broadened its customer base and became involved in the development of several diverse business and product opportunities, including health care products, plastic recycling, specialty compound development, and leisure products. In 1997, we built a much larger custom office and laboratory space across the street which houses the current PTI headquarters and laboratories, and which has been further expanded several times to accommodate the company's continued evolution.

The excursions outside the PET packaging field provided a basis for PTI to hire additional experienced technical professionals, to staff its laboratories, and to establish a reputation in the plastics industry as a substantial technical development company. In addition, diversifying the business provided PTI with the opportunity to learn more about technical product and business development.

PTI Headquarters at Wolf Creek Executive Park built in 1997 - 2021

In the end, however, PTI reconfirmed that its longer-term opportunities were in the PET technology business and today, while we still engage in an array of diverse plastics packaging industry technologies, our expertise and resources have been best focused on establishing PTI as the number one independent PET technology development and technical service resource in the world.

2015 PTI Companies Senior Management Team

Standing; Frank Schloss, Jim Sheely, Scott Steele, Thierry Fabozzi, Donald Miller
Sitting: Tracy Momany, Tom Brady, Betsy Brady

PTI Today

Today, **PTI** is recognized as a premiere PET technical development and support resource in the packaging industry.

Our 36 years of success has only been possible because of great people, starting with the key early team of Bob Deardurff, Scott Steele, Frank Semersky, and Betsy Brady, and continuing with the hundreds of owners, employees, and engineering co-op students who have followed and charted new paths since.

Together, we founded three successful sister companies that are still going strong including **Phoenix Technologies International, PTI-Europe,** and **Preform Technologies**. We also founded or co-founded several joint venture companies with industry partners including **INOVA Plastics, The Packaging Conference, Guardian Medical USA, Plastic Recovery Systems, Portare Leisure Products, PetWall LLC, Minus Nine Plastics,** and **PTI International**. We created 2 proprietary product businesses including **PTI Instruments** and **PT Healthcare Products**. We developed and/or licensed, sold, or used internally 18 proprietary products, including **Steel Coil Protective Rings, PortaBar™, Tru-Container™, StrataSys™ 3D Printer Material, OxyTraq™, TorqTraQ™, VisiTraQ™, LMS™, MuCell™, oPTI™ Foam Bottles, Virtual Prototyping™, PetWall Profiler™, Smart Blow Molding™, NFA™, PED2000™, SuperGreen™, LNOc™, LNOf™,** and the **Phoenix Process™**.

We are proud to have PTI employee names on more than 150 US and international patents, and we have served virtually every major PET machine and resin supplier, every major US food and beverage brand owner, and we have done business in more than 25 countries around the world.

PTI employees have delivered more than 200 papers and been sponsors at major technical and business conferences, including at the International Society of Beverage Technologists, the Plastics Institute of America, the National Plastics Exposition, and the Society of Plastic Engineers ANTEC Conference, and PTI has been instrumental in the startup and evolution of many of today's technical trade associations, including the Association of Plastic Recyclers, Polymer Ohio, and the Toledo Society of Plastic Engineers.

PTI offers a complete array of technical services, including product design, prototyping, and testing, with a complete materials and product analytical testing laboratory, and extensive lab-scale recycling capabilities. PTI also offers manufacturing support services and plastics education and training programs to the industry, and PTI's completely virtual product design and simulation capability has been employed across many industries and for customers who come to PTI specifically to develop and innovate new products.

Through the years, PTI and the PTI Family of Companies have expanded from a one-person office at the corner of Canton and Speilbusch Avenues in downtown Toledo in 1986, to its first rented office and laboratory facility at 333 14th Street in 1987, to our new 10,000 sq ft HQ building at Wolf Creek Executive Park in 1994, followed quickly by our now 52,000 sq ft HQ office/laboratory/storage facility in 1996, also in Wolf Creek, and which is owned by PTI employees. Along the way, facilities were added in Bowling Green, OH, Swanton, OH, and Yverdon Switzerland, adding a range of different capabilities.

PTI and PTI employees have also been important contributors to a great many community projects and organizations over our history. PTI remains an important supporter of the University of Toledo and the UT College of Engineering, where many PTI employees and co-op engineering students have trained over the years.

In 2021 PTI, PTI-Europe, and PTI Operations embarked on an exciting future as we became the US and European technical partner with SIPA Industries, one of the leading and most innovative packaging equipment and service providers in the world and a long-time PTI ally. SIPA is headquartered in Italy and will now offer PTI sales and service opportunities around the world.

Design

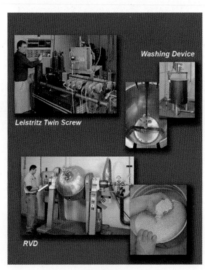

Process

Test

Today PTI offers Training and Education

Computer Design and Simulation

 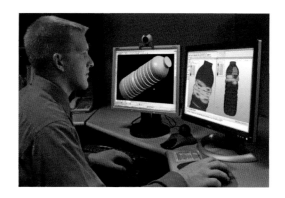

State-of-the-Art Prototyping and Processing

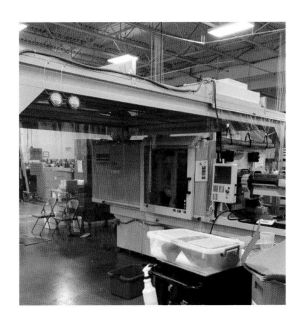

Analytical Material and Product Testing

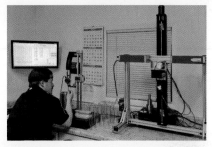

Specialty Instrumentation Development

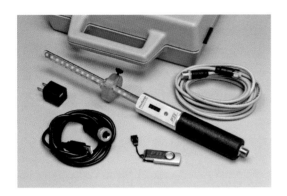

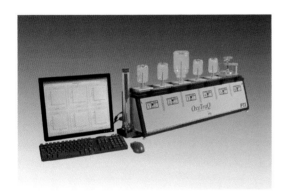

....and PTI has produced more than 150 US and international patents for PTI and for PTI customers.

PTI offers an attractive work environment for PTI employees and for PTI customers who regularly come to work in our labs.

PTI employees have developed thousands of packages and containers for customers around the world for the past 36 years.....

Handled bottles

First O-I Bottle and Preform - 1976

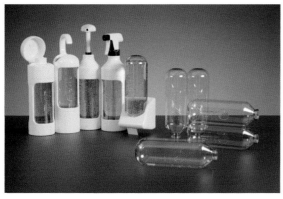

Dromo™ Shippable Packaging

Award winning Mountain Dew Package

oPTI™ Foam Technology

Special Promotional Packages

Bottles, Preforms, and Blow Mold

Cold Fill Bottles

Hot Fill Bottles and Preforms

Specialty Packaging

Proprietary oPTI™ Foam Technology

Integral Handle Features

Package in a Package

Recycle content containers

Packages Designed by PTI

FiCel ™ Technology

Wine Containers and Glasses

Award Winning Package Designs

oPTI ™ Foaming Technology

From Shampoos to Toothpaste

Household and Personal Care Containers with Recycle Content

Oriented Polypropylene Containers

Tervis™ Insulated Containers made from Tritan™ Copolyester Resin

Single Serve Packaging

Capsule Packaging

3D Printed Containers and Models

Ameristar Package of the Year Award

Aerosol Containers

Polypropylene Capsules

Grip Features

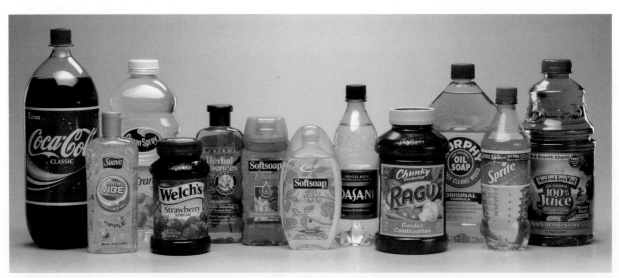

PTI Packages

..... and PTI regularly participates in the important international plastics conferences and expos!

Plastics Expo Display

PTI Trade Show Display

The Packaging Conference

Phoenix Technologies Trade Show Display

PTI Trade Show Display

Pack Expo Chicago 2019

The PTI Family of Companies

TO VIEW CLICK THE TOPIC BELOW

SERVICES & CAPABILITIES

PLASTIC TECHNOLOGIES, INC.

PHOENIX TECHNOLOGIES INTERNATIONAL LLC

PREFORM TECHNOLOGIES LLC

VIRTUAL PROTOTYPING™ MODULES

PET DRYING & MATERIAL HANDLING

INJECTION MOLD TROUBLESHOOTING

BLOW MOLD TROUBLESHOOTING

PET & PEN RESIN SPECIFICATIONS

PET PHYSICAL CONSTANTS

WE PACKAGE SOLUTIONS®

Phoenix Technologies International (a PTI Company)

Website: https://phoenixtechnologies.net/

Bob and Sue Deardurff,
Don and Mary Jane Hayward

PTI "intrapreneurs" who created and ran Phoenix Technologies include Bob Deardurff, PTI VP and Phoenix Technologies CEO, and Don Hayward, PTI Senior Technical Associate and first General Manager of Phoenix.

Other former O-I/PTI personnel who also assumed major operational roles at Phoenix Technologies include Jack Ritchie, Plant Superintendent, Henry Schworm, Chief Technical Officer, and Dennis Balduff, Principal Engineer.

Jack Ritchie

Operations executives who were important to the success of Phoenix include Ron Ott, Plant Manager and President, Jean Bina, Operations Manager, Steve Schultz, Finance Manager, Elaine Canning, Chief Financial Officer, Shari McCague, Corporate Accountant, and Lori Carson, Sales & Marketing Manager, Operations Director, and Site Manager.

Jean Bina & Dennis Balduff

Elaine Canning

Shari McCague.

Henry Schworm

The Phoenix Technologies Team!

Lori Carson

Phoenix Technologies was established in 1992 and is now recognized as a global leader in recycled PET (RPET). The company manufactures clean, consistent, high-grade RPET resin pellets from post-consumer recycled plastic shipped from all over the world.

PET Bottles Containing up to 100% RPET

As a premier manufacturer of RPET, Phoenix sets the benchmark for quality, technology, service, and overall value. Phoenix's 90,000 square foot, state-of-the-art, Ohio recycling facility was designed from the ground up and produces 80 million pounds of RPET annually.

Using a fine-mesh filtration process or a fine-ground powder process, Phoenix can produce RPET which exceeds the industry's highest standards. Additionally, Phoenix RPET can be used along with virgin bottle resins to create bottles with the right attributes for any

application. Phoenix Technologies is ISO certified and is continuously introducing new technologies and equipment, enabling it to supply high quality RPET for both food and non-food applications.

By using patented technologies in combination with proprietary blending methods and fine mesh melt filtration systems, Phoenix produces the highest-quality recycled PET (RPET) that customers have come to expect over the past two decades.

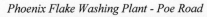

Phoenix Flake Washing Plant - Poe Road

Phoenix Pelletizing Plant - Fairview Avenue

Phoenix prides itself on having ultra clean facilities, manufacturing quality products, and having an impeccable safety record. More than a manufacturer, Phoenix thinks of itself as a partner to brand owners and to converters. By leveraging Phoenix's strategic alliances with resin manufacturers, colorant and additive suppliers, processors, bottle producers, and sheet extruders, Phoenix can give its customers a competitive advantage.

In June, 2019, Taiwan-based Far Eastern New Century Corp. (FENC) announced the acquisition of Phoenix Technologies International LLC, Bowling Green, Ohio.

Phoenix is the third production site FENC has acquired in the U.S. over the last several years, including a PET production plant in West Virginia, a research and development center in Ohio and another PET plant in Texas.

Because governments around the world have enacted regulations that require businesses to increase the proportion of recycled raw materials in their products and considering the strong demand for green products in the U.S. market, this acquisition will help FENC's downstream global beverage brand and consumer product clients meet those sustainable development goals. FENC believes that the acquisition of Phoenix will help it to solidify the synergy with its subsidiary in West Virginia as well.

FENC is the world's second largest recycled PET producer and the third largest virgin PET resin supplier. Since 1988, FENC has been conducting R&D on the manufacturing process of recycling and its applications. Its recycling facilities are in Taiwan, Japan, the Philippines, and in the U.S.

PTI-Europe SARL (a PTI Company)

PTI-Europe was established in 1998 and initially operated as a separate but wholly owned PTI company in Lausanne, Switzerland for the purpose of conducting package and materials development projects for PTI customers located in Europe. In 2003, PTI-Europe moved from Lausanne to Yverdon-les-Bains, Switzerland and expanded its Analytical Laboratory, adding a joint venture permeability testing laboratory with MOCON Corporation.

Shortly after the move, PTI-Europe added a Recycled PET Laboratory which is available to the industry, and PTI-Europe's PET Technology Training Program is now recognized as a standard industry training program for the European PET industry.

Frank Semersky, Helene Lanctuit, Jean-Claude Baumgartner, Christian Ducreux, Beatrice, Yen Andenmatten, Anne Roulin

Jean-Claude Baumgartner, Sylvie Vaucher, Vincent Le Guen, Yen Andenmatten, Helene Lanctuit, Christian Ducreux

PTI "intrapreneurs" who created and managed PTI – Europe SARL include the late Frank Semersky, PTI VP New Business Development, and Anne Roulin, the first General Manager of PTI-Europe.

Despite the smaller size of the European operation, PTI-E was nevertheless able to bring several innovations to the market and to establish strong relationships with several key global brand owners. One of these early key developments was the first commercial re-heat stretch blow molded PP bottle in Europe, carried out in collaboration with P&G and LyondellBasell Industries, one of the largest plastics, chemicals, and refining companies in the world.

The Deep-Grip bottle was another key development carried out for P&G, where PTI-Europe not only developed the entire concept at the lab scale but managed the development of the required industrial machinery with Sidel.

PTI-Europe also had a major role in the development and qualification of PET recycling technologies, initially by supporting Petcore Europe, the trade association representing the complete PET value chain in Europe since 1993, and by supporting the EPBP (European PET Bottle Platform) organization as a certified testing laboratory. In 2012 PTI-Europe became the first external Mocon Certified Testing Facility

Dana Giorgerini

Christian Ducreux, Greg Fisher, Nicolas Sframeli

When Thierry Fabozzi came from Nestlé to assume the General Manager's role in 2012, he added the thin-wall molding and single serve capsule technologies to PTI-Europe's capabilities. Today Thierry is the President and CEO of the PTI Companies.

Dana Giorgerini, Scott Steele, Stéphane Morier, Thierry Fabozzi, Antonio Farré, Pascal Sandoz, Nicolas Sframeli, Matthieu Larose, Jean-Claude Baumgartner, Christian Ducreux, Florence Baroni, Jean-Luc Roulin, Greg Fisher, Yen Andenmatten, Sylvie Magnin

The Packaging Conference (a PTI joint venture company)

Website: https://thepackagingconference.com

PTI "intrapreneurs" who created and ran the Packaging Conference include the late Frank Semersky, then PTI VP New Business Development and Ron Puvak, then PTI Marketing and Sales Director. PTI's Packaging Conference joint venture partner initially was SBA-CCI, founded by John Maddox, a former technical executive at Eastman Chemical, one of the industry's premier PET resin suppliers.

The Packaging Conference was created in 2008 as a joint venture between PTI and SBA-CCI as an annual industry conference that would update industry packaging professionals on the latest innovations in technology, design, and sustainability. Over the years, industry leaders from across the packaging supply chain, including consumer packaging suppliers, resin suppliers, technology providers, equipment manufacturers, and container, closure, and label manufacturers have gathered to facilitate connections and to share the latest consumer packaging innovations.

Networking Opportunities

The Packaging Conference exhibit area is always the focal point for investigating new technologies, businesses, and ideas. Each of the breakfasts, the morning and afternoon refreshment breaks, the Monday evening reception, and Tuesday luncheon are all designed for maximum networking.

In 2020 SBA-CCI became the sole owner of The Packaging Conference, although PTI continues to support what has become the number one annual packaging industry forum.

PTI Operations / Preform Technologies, Inc.

Website: http://www.preformtechnologies.com/

PTI "intrapreneurs" who created and managed PTI Operations (initially, Preform Technologies) include Bob Deardurff, Dan Durham, and Jim Sheely.

Preform Technologies, LLC (PTLLC) was formed in late 2003 as a manufacturing company that provides specialty and niche PET preforms and bottles and offers specialty injection molding services for other packaging applications.

In effect, PTI Operations is the extended production arm of Plastic Technologies, Inc. When customers require additional preform or bottle capacity over and above prototyping quantities, PTI Operations supplies those production and pre-production quantities. PTI Operations also specializes in supporting new product market launches and supplies customer special product requirements, including specialty colors or materials.

While PTI Operations, PTI, and Phoenix Technologies can offer design, development, production, and recycle-content preforms and bottles which customers can't get anywhere else from a single source, customers may also order capacities directly from PTI Operations, when those customers have no capacity in house or because the needed quantities are too small to make the customer's own production worthwhile.

PTI Operations focuses exclusively on supplying specialty packaging, not just commodity items, and the installed injection and blow molding technology for preforms can also be used to manufacture other injection and blow molded parts, in addition to preforms for bottles.

The fleet of PTI Operations machines includes Husky and SIPA injection machines, Sidel SBO and SIPA stretch blow-molding machines, Nissei Single Stage Injection/Blow molding machines, and Bekum extrusion blow molding machines.

As one of the <u>PTI Global</u> family of companies, PTI Operations has an experienced technical team supporting PTI's efforts worldwide. PTI Operations' portfolio includes a long list of PET and polyolefin preform and container success stories.

Having been the silent partner for many key packaging innovations, PTI Operations knows how important confidentiality, performance, and speed are to all customers.

PTI Operations offers a variety of process and product capabilities that can propel customers all the way from "concept to commercialization," and utilizing PTI Operations as a key independent development resource allows customers to take advantage of a variety of tooling and machine capabilities, without having to make a capital investment.

Over its 18 year history, PTI Operations has established itself as the premier manufacturer of technically challenging PET preforms, and also specializes in producing smaller volume PET and polyolefin preforms for food, personal care and other applications. Additionally, PTI Operations can provide smaller quantity runs of injection, extrusion, or reheat stretch-blow-molded containers.

PTI Operations' extensive capabilities also can be used for emergencies or for smaller preform runs when customers don't want to disrupt their own production, including assisting with:

- Production quantities - technically challenging preform production.
- Resin trials - multiple materials and small run volumes.
- Test market quantities - 500,000 to 5 million preforms.
- Overflow volumes - 10 to 20 million preforms per year via predictable monthly draws.
- Emergency runs - unforeseen and emergency supply issues.
- Container production - small quantity runs of injection, extrusion or reheat stretch blow-molded containers using PET, PP, HDPE and other resins.

Guardian Medical USA

Toledo Mayor Michael Bell, Tom Brady, Betsy Brady, UT President Dr. Lloyd Jacobs, UT Engineering Dean Dr. Nagi Naganathan

UT Professor of Bioengineering Dr. VJ Goel, Renowned Spinal Surgeon and Founder of Spinal Balance Dr. Anand Agarwal, Tom & Betsy Brady, PTI Chief Technical Officer Tracy Momany, ProMedica CEO Randy Oostra

In 2017 after I was finished judging the University of Toledo College of Engineering Freshman Design Competition presentations which took place in the Brady Engineering Innovation Center at the University of Toledo, I was approached by Dr. Anand Agarwal who I had never met before and who asked if I was interested in learning about a new plastic packaging development that Dr. Agarwal and his team at Spinal Balance, a startup medical device company, were pursuing. Spinal Balance was in UT's Entrepreneurship Incubator in the same building as the Brady Engineering Innovation Center so, my answer was an instant "for sure," and off we went to see what Spinal Balance was all about.

As an experienced and world-renowned spinal surgeon, Dr. Agarwal realized that regulators, insurance providers, and hospitals were driving a transition from the standard industry practice of using orthopedic implants that must be sterilized before each procedure, to implant systems that were prepackaged in a sterile condition, to decrease risk, reduce costs, and meet changing regulatory requirements. As these requirements were just beginning to take effect, the entire industry was being forced to replace the then-current non-sterile and unlabeled implants with packaged sterile implants.

Dr. Agarwal explained that sterile tube packaging virtually eliminates the risk of seal failures, saves inventory space, is intuitive to use, and saves surgical time as well as providing the required traceability of individual parts from the time of manufacture to patient delivery by using a Unique Device Identification (UDI).

As we considered the opportunity, we learned that the global market for medical implant sterile packaging was already valued at $1.5 billion and was expected to grow to $2.7 billion by 2025, and that even though there were already several sterile package suppliers for orthopedic implants, sterile "tube packaging" for orthopedic implants was the trend, and that Dr. Agarwal and Spinal Balance had just developed and applied for patents on a unique and (he believed) superior sterile medical tube packaging design.

However, Dr. Agarwal also realized that Spinal Balance did not have the plastics expertise to develop and manufacture his proprietary sterile packaging, but after hearing me talk about plastic manufacture during the judging competition, he correctly concluded that perhaps PTI and Spinal Balance could form a joint venture company to produce Spinal Balance's patented sterile packaging, which is exactly what we did!

Of course, PTI had no expertise or contacts in the medical industry, even though we knew there was huge opportunity in medical packaging, and Spinal Balance had no expertise in plastic package design and manufacture, even though that is what Dr. Agarwal needed to commercialize his ideas!

Within a matter of several months, we got to know each other, and we agreed to form a joint venture company to design and manufacture the proprietary packaging for Spinal Balance, and for the industry generally.

We named our new company Guardian Medical USA and located the new company in space leased from PTI's Preform Technologies LLC manufacturing company which had both injection and blow molding capacity, and we contracted with PTI to do all the design and prototyping of our developing product lines.

Guardian designed and installed a clean room and quickly got up to speed on the rigors of FDA approvals which, of course, was where Spinal Balance's medical product experience was essential.

Tracy Momany, a 30-year seasoned expert in plastic package development and the former Chief Technical Officer at PTI is CEO and Betsy Brady, a PTI Founder is Chairman of the Board. Don Kennedy, with 40 years of experience in the medical industry, is VP of Sales and is contacting medical device companies seeking sales opportunities. Natalie Holobaugh, with prior operating experience at Amazon, is the Operations Manager and has been instrumental in the creation of Guardian's quality control and production systems.

Sales and numbers of customers are projected to grow rapidly and the goal of finding a strategic buyer within the medical industry looks extremely promising. As of this writing, the Guardian leadership team has secured additional venture capital investment funding which will move this startup to the next level.

Advantages of Tube Packaging

Less waste, easier package access, more space efficiency, improved user safety, and better labeling

 VS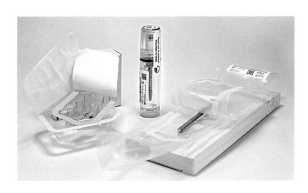

 VS

We Package Solutions®

New (PET Technology) Business Development

As PTI continued to grow and to provide technical development services to virtually all companies involved in PET packaging including brand owners, converters, resin suppliers, machinery manufacturers and raw material suppliers, PTI professionals developed several exciting and high potential technologies which were owned by PTI, and which offered potential sales or licensing opportunities.

To take advantage of these proprietary technologies, PTI created a New Business Development activity having the charter to pursue internal technology developments as business opportunities, either by joint venture, or by licensing, or by creating independent companies.

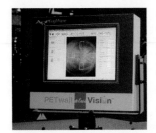

As a result, in 2001 PTI identified Non-Contact International (NCI) as a joint venture partner with the goal of developing a commercial prototype for an on-line bottle wall thickness measurement technology developed and patented by PTI. The joint venture partners, PTI and NCI, formed a separate licensing company, PETWall LLC, which completed the development of the wall thickness gauge and licensed the technology to a global supplier of on-line inspection equipment, Agr-TopWave.

Today, Agr-TopWave manufactures, sells, and services online plastic bottle inspection equipment, trade-named **PETWall Vision™** which utilizes the original **PETWall™** wall thickness gauging systems technology.

Those early relationships between PTI and its partners spurred the development of additional instrumentation products, including **TorqTraQ™**, a hand-held closure removal torque meter, **WallTraQ™**, a wall thickness gauge, **VacTraQ™**, a vacuum resistance meter, and **OxyTraQ™**, an oxygen permeation system which was licensed to MOCON for manufacture and sale as another instrument in the MOCON product line.

TorqTraQ ™   *WallTraQ ™*   *VacTraQ ™*   *OxyTraQ ™*

In 2003 PTI formed a joint venture with Container Consulting Inc. (CCI) for the purpose of commercializing and licensing another PTI proprietary technology to the industry. **Virtual Prototyping (VP)™** is a computer simulation of PET preform/bottle design and processing which allows the user to optimize the design of a preform and bottle combination prior to prototyping, by simulating the reheat-blow molding process using a computer-designed preform and then iterating the initial preform design by predicting the final bottle material distribution and performance. This very powerful **VP™** software offers the industry higher speed and accuracy for routine bottle design and development and is now available for license from either CCI or from PTI.

oPTI™ foamed PET technology was developed and patented by PTI but a partnership with Ferromatik/Milacron (injection machines) and Foboha (injection molds) was essential to develop the needed commercial overmolding system. This unique and proprietary technology was featured at NPE and then transferred to Preform Technologies where production samples were made for customers. Coca-Cola successfully test-marketed the technology in Europe, but it was never introduced in the US because of cost

Other technologies developed by PTI include the **NFA Leak Monitor™,** a bottle imperfection detector which uses an ultrasonic method to "hear" defects as they are created during the blow molding process, a **Laser Measurement System (LMS™)**, which automatically creates a complete map of the outer dimensions of a bottle using laser detection of the outside surface in three-dimensional space, and a preform "free-blow" device for the laboratory, the **PED-2000™**, which allows the user to quickly and accurately determine "natural stretch ratio" for any bottle-making resin. PTI built and sold these internally developed electronic systems as PTI products, but we also licensed the **NFA Leak Monitor™** to **ALPS Inspection**, a **TSAI** company that manufactures and sells in-line leak detection systems to the packaging industry (https://www.alpsleak.com).

Industry Publications Documenting PTI's Businesses

Entrepreneurial Spirit Molds Plastic Technologies' Success

Published in Industry Week Magazine, Sept 2, 2015

By Michele Nash-Hoff

https://www.industryweek.com/leadership/companies-executives/article/22008099/entrepreneurial-spirit-molds-plastic-technologies-success

Plastic Technologies was built on technical expertise, but speed and efficiency are becoming increasingly important in a more competitive environment.

During a recent tour of manufacturing plants in the Toledo region, I decided to write an article about <u>Plastic Technologies,</u> Inc because of the interesting story about Dr. Tom Brady who founded the company in 1985. Brady worked for Owens-Illinois, Inc. from 1971-1984 and became Vice President and Director of Plastics Technology.

He led the development of the first PET (polyester) plastic soft drink container and directed the technical activities for all O-I's plastic product lines.

Asked what led him to start PTI, he said, "In late 1985, I happened upon a unique opportunity to start the company. Several of the major Coca-Cola bottlers were seeking to expand their already successful PET bottle manufacturing operations and to develop new and innovative PET plastic soft drink packaging products. The four largest Coca-Cola regional bottling cooperatives agreed to jointly sponsor and fund product development and engineering projects, and they approached me to manage those project development efforts.

Not having an interest in just changing jobs, I made a counteroffer to those Coca-Cola cooperatives to establish a separate independent company for the purpose of managing their projects. When they agreed, I left O-I to start Plastic Technologies, Inc. and signed long-term contracts with all four Coca-Cola cooperatives.

"Because of my industry experience, I was quickly able to identify additional customers that were non-competitive to Coca-Cola, and I hired a small but highly experienced professional staff to do the technical development for the Coca-Cola cooperatives and for other customers," Brady continued.

"Because of our professionalism and experience, we were quickly able to establish a reputation in the industry as a high-quality PET R&D and technical support company.

"As our technical staff expanded and our revenue grew at compound annual rates of 35%, we moved to a larger facility in 1989 and set up both analytical testing and process development laboratories, with the capability of prototyping and testing PET containers and preforms. We founded Phoenix Technologies International LLC in 1991 in nearby Bowling Green, Ohio and have since then expanded the plant three times to produce recycled PET using proprietary technology."

"Because PET had become the material of choice for new packaging during the 80s and 90s, we were able to quickly expand our customer base and to become involved in developing many different products and businesses, including health care packaging, plastic recycling, specialty compound development and even leisure products. Our experiences outside the PET packaging field provided a basis for us to hire additional technical professionals to staff our laboratories and establish a reputation in the plastics industry as a substantial technical development company.

"Since those early days, we have developed relationships with most major manufacturers, resin suppliers, machinery builders, brand owners, and converters. Today, we even supply preforms for blow molding to customers needing specific quantities or unusual designs. We have also learned how to work effectively with competitive customers, and we have become recognized for our excellence in protecting customer intellectual property and confidentiality. Today, our customers are involved in every step of the PET value chain from raw material supply through end-of-life recyclability."

I asked if they were affected by the recession of 2008-2009 and if so, what did they do to survive it? Brady said, "The recession did have a big effect on PTI's business, but the recession, per se, was not the most significant issue. Rather, the recession just added to the challenge of changes that were already happening in the world at large."

As is true for almost every business today, one of the challenges for PTI today is to redefine its business going forward. Brady said that what PTI has done successfully for 30 years is no longer as different and special as it once was. The challenge for PTI, and for every business today, is to find the "gaps" in the markets of the future that can be filled by employing the experience and knowledge that has been developed over many years.

Brady did say "We had to do some things differently during the recession. We had to get more professional about sales because there are many more companies selling the same technologies and services now. The biggest impediment to our continued growth is that there are more competitors, so that staying ahead of the competition is a bigger challenge." When he started the company, he was working with the top levels of management at his major customers. Now, he says that business is being done at a different level. More business is handled today by professional purchasing agents, so you must be more price competitive than in the past. They also went through formal training in Lean, which has been beneficial to their manufacturing businesses, because, he says, "You have to be more efficient to be competitive in every aspect of your business today." However, the Lean initiative didn't affect PTI's testing lab, where becoming ISO certified had more of an impact.

Since I had seen a whole wall of patents PTI had been granted on display at their headquarters, I asked if the change in patent law under the America Invents Act of 2011 affected his company. He replied, "We have to take the steps to be 'first to file' instead of being able to rely on being 'first to invent.' We must file more provisional patents than we ever had to in the past, which adds another big burden and costs that we didn't have previously. Our number of patent applications has shrunk now that we can't depend on being first to invent. Anything that adds bureaucratic activity becomes a burden on business."

After my visit, I had emailed Brady information on the proposed patent legislation (H.R. 9 and S.1137) and asked if these bills would have an effect on his company. He responded, "You don't have time to fight everything that comes up. You try to work around it. In fact, we find that patents are less valuable than they used to be. It is more important to be first to the market and to be innovative. Our growth hasn't been about becoming a bigger and bigger company. We started Phoenix Technologies and our other companies so that those teams could be more entrepreneurial themselves. Our growth model has been to expand by creating our own 'Intrapreneurs,' by offering those intrapreneurs ownership and by growing as a family of companies."

"Our PTI family of companies now includes two manufacturing companies, two technical development and engineering service companies and three joint venture companies that license technology or sell specialty services to the packaging industry (Preform Technologies LLC, Phoenix Technologies International LLC, PTI Europe SARL, PETWall LLC, Minus 9 Plastics LLC and The Packaging Conference). Today, many PTI employees are owners and are in a position where they can truly feel it's their company."

"Any employee can be considered by the management team for an opportunity to buy an equity stake, and 40% of PTI employees are owners today. We have more than 200 employees worldwide and many of the products you buy every day are sold in plastic containers designed by one of our companies."

During my visit, I was astonished to learn that there are only 10 states that have bottle deposit programs to encourage recycling — California, Connecticut, Delaware, Hawaii, Iowa, Maine, Massachusetts, Michigan, New York, Oregon, and Vermont. In these states, about 80% of bottles are recycled, while in non-bottle-deposit states only about 20% of bottles are recycled.

Asked why more states don't have bottle deposit programs, Brady responded that "many major companies oppose the programs because they say it would add to their costs."

He explained, "You have to have an infrastructure in place to get enough material to make recycling profitable." However, he emphasized that everybody, even those who think deposit systems cost more money, would win if there was more recycled material, because the costs for virgin material would go down. He also pointed out that a lot of the recycled material goes offshore to China and other Asian countries because it is cheaper to ship the material in the empty containers that are going back to Asia than it is to ship the material to Ohio.

"We are a big enough company that we can buy recycled material from other sources in Mexico, Canada, South America, and even Iceland; and we also benefit because we put it back into the highest value end-use products — food and beverage containers," said Brady, who pointed out that when China and India get to our standard of living, there isn't going to be enough of all the raw materials to go around.

That means that reusing all materials will eventually become necessary and that recycling will become a significant industry, rather than remaining a "nice thing to do."

In 2009, Brady took a leave of absence from the company to become the interim dean of Education at the University of Toledo. He said, "At first, I was judged by the faculty and staff at the college to be a poor choice as the interim dean. However, I had the advantage of being completely dependent upon the expertise and experience of the faculty and staff at the college. I made a personal commitment to get to know each and every person in the college and to understand the personal and professional backgrounds of everyone. As a result, we were able to work together to craft a mission and strategy for the future and to create a climate of success going forward."

Therefore, I wasn't surprised to learn that Brady's grandfather founded the University of Toledo's College of Secondary Education. His mother, an aunt, his two sisters and his grandmother all taught school. He doesn't just "talk the talk," he "walks the talk." When he was interviewed by <u>Plastic News</u> prior to being inducted into the Society of Plastics Industry Hall of Fame in, 2012, he said, "My goal is to help anywhere I can to make education better. If we don't educate our kids in this country, we're lost."

"Our only competitive advantage is being able to be entrepreneurs. The rest of the world can catch up in everything else, so we better figure it out. And there are not going to be enough unskilled jobs in the future, so you better educate people so they can go out and create their own jobs."

Dr. Brady emphasized the importance of education and training to economic development. "In a sense, I think I could reduce the entire economic development issue to just this one issue. That is, if we spent every one of our economic development dollars on building a world class PreK-20 education and training system, I truly believe that economic development would happen naturally as a by-product of that initiative."

He reiterated a point that he had made to the Mayor of Toledo a few years earlier:

- Higher per-capita income is a by-product of higher-paying jobs
- Higher-paying jobs are a by-product of knowledge-based commerce
- Knowledge-based commerce is a by-product of education and talent
- Talent and education are by-products of a superior K-16 school system, substantive trade and skill development institutions, and a superior teaching and research university.

I completely concur and made similar points in my book, "Can American Manufacturing be Saved?" Why we should and how we can, as well as the several blog articles I have written about workforce development and attracting the next generation of manufacturing workers.

Manufacturing jobs are the foundation of our economy and the middle class. We must strengthen our manufacturing industry to create more jobs if we want our children and grandchildren to have an opportunity to live the "American Dream."

Toledo-based PTI Leads Plastic Packaging, Recycling Industries

Published in 2009 by The Toledo Free Press
Written by Duane Ramsey, Senior Business Writer
news@toledofreepress.com

A Toledo group of companies known as PTI develops plastic packaging and plastic package recycling for major companies like Coca-Cola and Colgate-Palmolive.

Plastic Technologies Inc. (PTI) and the family of companies are a privately-owned business that develops plastic containers for Coca-Cola and for Colgate and for many other consumer product companies at its Toledo headquarters, where it conducts research and develops manufacturing processes.

Another PTI company, Phoenix Technologies International, is the world's largest producer of recycled plastic resins used in the production of clean plastic bottles and containers for Coca-Cola, Colgate and for other customers, PTI officials said.

It all began in the 1980s when a young plastics engineer named Tom Brady was asked to develop plastic bottles for Coca-Cola. While serving as Vice President of Plastics Technology at Owens-Illinois Inc., Brady led the development of the first plastic soft containers made of polyethylene terephthalate, known as PET, now the most recycled plastic packaging material in the world.

When O-I decided not to invest in the plastic container business at that time, Brady took the proverbial leap of faith, left O-I and started PTI in 1985. Today, PTI employs more than 200 people worldwide and is the leading PET packaging development resource in the industry.

"When it comes to PET containers, PTI is the premier development company and has clients around the world. That speaks very highly of their expertise in that industry," said Dr. Saleh Jabarin, director of the University of Toledo College of Engineering Polymer Institute.

Jabarin and Brady were colleagues in plastics technology at O-I and were also undergraduate classmate students at Dartmouth College. After Brady left O-I, he helped Jabarin establish the UT Polymer Institute which involved moving the entire O-I Plastic Development Laboratory to UT.

It's not the only connection PTI has with the UT. Brady said that 4 of the company's 7 vice presidents and a third of all its employees are graduates of business, engineering, or science programs at UT.

Brady also serves on the UT Board of Trustees and chairs the External Affairs Committee, which oversees technology transfer and commercialization. He also sits on the Ohio governor's Third Frontier Advisory Board and on the board of directors of the Regional Growth Partnership, SSOE Inc., Toledo School for the Arts and the Toledo Symphony.

Brady says that "The secret to corporate success is hiring people who are smarter than you and then getting out of their way." He also says and believes that "Entrepreneurial activity is not about having everything laid out in front of you. Rather, it's about taking the playing field you have and then making something out of it."

Brady says that "You must have a strategic plan but, you must also go where the business takes you. You must diversify while specializing and while also adding intellectual capacity. Our success has also been about building a business that provides full-service and unparalleled knowledge and we have focused on offering the shortest response time in the plastic packaging industry."

PTI developed the first plastic bottle for Coca-Cola and has designed all subsequent plastic containers for Coca-Cola, Brady said. The combined PTI companies provide research, development, design and prototyping capabilities for Coca-Cola, Colgate, and for many other household and industrial product users.

One of PTI's companies, Perform Technologies LLC, manufactures small-to-medium production runs of plastic bottles and containers at its Toledo facility. Preform Technologies also produces specialty injection-molded packaging products and pre-forms for bottle manufacturing.

As another service to the industry, PTI also develops equipment, instruments, and provides manufacturing support and training to the plastic packaging industry.

PTI-Europe, located in Yverdon les Bains, Switzerland, provides the same plastic development services and products to Coca-Cola and to other PTI clients in Europe. And PTI also operates two investment and technology licensing companies to support its other businesses.

Most recently, PTI formed The Packaging Conference LLC, a joint venture company which will sponsor annual international conferences for the packaging industry. Brady said the first conference was hosted Feb. 4 in Las Vegas, which attracted 180 persons from 100 companies.

Brady said PTI is in the process of a management/ownership transition that will result in him and his wife, Betsy, vice president of finance, administration, and chief financial officer, maintaining 40 percent ownership with its officers and employees owning the remaining 60 percent of the company.

PTI's newest executive, Craig Barrow, recently joined the management team as Vice President and Chief Operating Officer, and will transition to President of PTI, when Brady becomes Interim Dean of Education at UT later this year.

"There is no shortage of innovation at PTI. Remarkable things are happening without any lack of imagination," he said.

PET Bottle Pioneer Brady Lends Imagination to Education

Published in Plastics News Magazine, April 2, 2012
Written by Bill Bregar

Thomas Brady, chairman of PET packaging research and development firm Plastic Technologies Inc., is full of creative ideas about plastic bottles — and the future of American education.

In 2009, Brady took a bold step for an industrialist. He accepted the invitation of University of Toledo President Lloyd Jacobs to become interim dean of UT's College of Education.

That level of community activism comes naturally for Brady. He also is active in Toledo schools, both public and charter, and serves on the boards of the Regional Growth Partnership Board and Ohio's Third Frontier program.

Oh, by the way ... his company helped create the contour PET Coca-Cola bottle, and other landmark packages.

Now Brady reaches another landmark, as he joins the Plastics Hall of Fame. The native of Maumee, Ohio, explained his wide-ranging interests in an interview at PTI in Holland, near Toledo.

Brady got in on the ground floor of PET soda bottles, joining Owens-Illinois Inc. in 1972 as senior scientist in plastic materials and processes. The three other PTI co-founders also worked at O-I: Scott Steele, named president earlier this year when Brady became chairman; Bob Deardurff, president of sister company Phoenix Technologies International LLC, a PET recycler; and Frank Semersky, who recently retired as vice president, New Business Development.

Steele nominated Brady for the Plastics Hall of Fame.

"I, along with Bob and Scott and a number of other people at Owens-Illinois, were literally responsible for starting up our manufacturing operations in the beverage business, between 1976 and 1984," Brady said. "Remember, O-I had never made PET bottles. It was a whole new business."

Brady earned a master's degree in materials science from Dartmouth College. After getting a doctorate from the University of Michigan in engineering plastics materials, he joined Owens-Illinois.

O-I was a whirlwind of activity. He helped set up its first PET blow molding plant, in Milford, Conn., followed by factories in Maryland, Alabama, California and Canada, all in a five-year period.

A major glass-container manufacturer, O-I was already into plastics, but it was all polyethylene, PVC and polystyrene bottles for household products. PET soda bottles were new and exotic.

"When I walked in, very quickly it was: How do you get stuff in machines and make bottles out of it? And that was the interesting thing. We went from being literally new engineers to experienced people in a matter of a few years, because there was nobody else. We went and did it. We invented the machines. We designed the bottles. We invented the processes."

Brady eventually rose to become Vice President and Director of R&D.

Meanwhile, led by John Dunagan, a Coca-Cola bottler in Texas, bottlers were setting up in-house blow molding. Eventually, several bottlers would become giants of self-manufacturing such as Western Container Corp., Southeastern Container Inc., Apple Container Corp. and FlorPak.

Dunagan offered Brady a job in 1984. Intrigued, he knew it was a pivotal moment since, as he said, "There were probably literally 10 people in the world that knew as much as I did about PET. How many times in your life do you end up being in the right place at the right time? But I really didn't want to go work for somebody else again."

Instead, Brady decided to leave Owens-Illinois and start his own firm. The first client: Coca-Cola Co. and the bottlers. PTI was born in 1985.

Early projects were multilayer PET containers with an ethylene vinyl alcohol barrier layer and a plastic soda can. Light weighting was a major push.

"We saved Coca-Cola millions and millions of dollars, just taking weight out of the preform," Brady said.

PTI began a long-term relationship with Colgate-Palmolive Co., designing its new PET containers for consumer staples like liquid hand soaps, laundry detergent and dishwashing liquid.

Today PTI has more than 200 customers. The company employs about 200 people, 100 of them in the Toledo area.

"This is really the premier provider of package technology and materials-development services for the industry. And we work for everybody," he said. PTI's walls are adorned with plaques detailing 140 patents.

Brady said PTI has kept its entrepreneurial roots. About 50 of the 200 employees have ownership stakes in PTI or its six sister companies, which include Phoenix Technologies, Preform Technologies LLC, PETWall LLC, Minus 9 Plastics LLC and The Packaging Conference.

The firm is active in bio-resins and nanotechnology.

Education: Walking the walk

Lots of business executives complain about America's education system. Brady gets directly involved.

"My goal is to help anywhere I can to make education better," he said. "If we don't educate our kids in this country, we're lost. Our only competitive advantage is being able to be entrepreneurs. The rest of the world can catch up in everything else, so we better figure it out. And if you hope you get a job at Chrysler, that's one thing. But if you educate people, they'll go out and create their own jobs."

His grandfather founded the University of Toledo's college of secondary education. His mother, an aunt, his two sisters and both grandmothers all taught school.

Toledo is one of the leaders in Ohio in vocational education, and Brady was a founding board member of the Toledo Technology Academy. PTI welcomes interns from the school.

Brady said he feels strongly that not everybody needs to go to college. But young people do need some post-secondary training. "There are lots of jobs out there — welding, machine technology, process controls, electrical technicians, computer technicians, you name it — that don't require four years of college."

He serves on the boards of Toledo Early College High School and the Toledo School for the Arts and his wife, Betsy, is a trustee and past chairman of the Toledo Museum of Art.

Tom Brady is active in a major effort in Toledo schools to create a STEM program (science, technology, engineering, and mathematics) all the way from kindergarten through high school.

Brady calls his two years as interim dean of UT's college of education "one of the most satisfying things I've ever done." At first, he had some doubts. So did the faculty.

"I was an engineer, not a guy from education. And they said, 'Here's a guy who's all about profit; we're about mission.' I mean, I had three strikes against me."

Brady left PTI to become dean in 2009 and 2010. He spent time getting to know the professors personally. He worked hard to meet all the area school superintendents. He made connections with local business leaders.

Brady thinks education can benefit from fresh thinking. Too often, the education establishment gets "inbred," he said. "It gets to be very defensive about itself," he said.

"One of the things that happens in the private sector is, there's lots of crossover. People go back and forth. You know what's going on in your industry and other industries. And what I became convinced of is, we need more people to get into education that haven't been in it."

Tom Brady's Home Plastic Packaging Museum

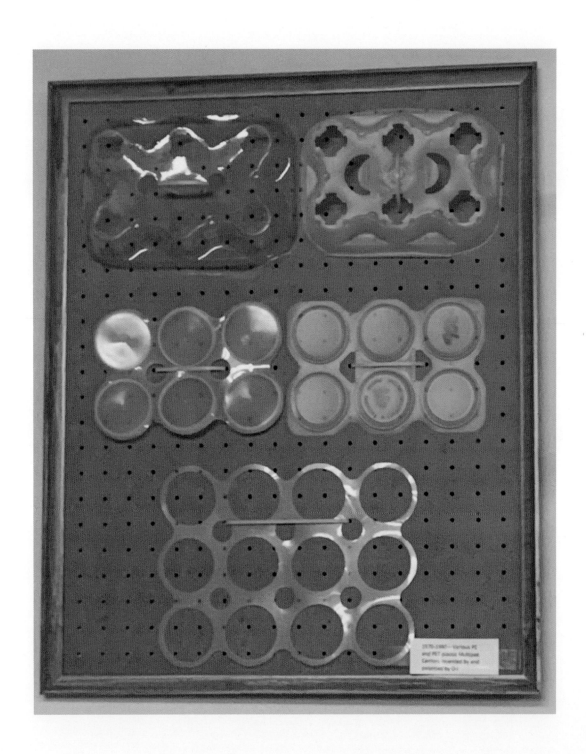

1970-1987 – Various PE
and PET pieces. Multipak
Carriers invented by and
patented by Ori

130

The Future - The Case for a Circular Economy

By Thomas E. Brady, PhD
August 2021
Information courtesy of The Sustainability Institute

A circular economy is restorative and regenerative by design. This means materials constantly flow around a 'closed loop' system, rather than being used once and then discarded. In the case of plastic, this means simultaneously keeping the value of plastics in the economy, without leakage into the natural environment. The Ellen MacArthur Foundation reported that more than 40 years after the launch of the first universal recycling symbol, just 14% of the plastic packaging used globally is recycled, while 40% ends up in landfill and 32% in ecosystems, with the remaining 14% used for incineration or energy recovery. To move society away from the "take, make, dispose" mindset that has long-informed business models, a fundamental rethinking is required which will involve a) improving recycling, b) promoting reuse, and c) creating a market for recycled materials and redesigning products with end of life in mind.

While it is true that "the future belongs to those who prepare for it today," I believe that the opportunity for the plastics industry is to support and create products and systems which will "incentivize the consumer and industry to participate."

Technologies and systems for reuse of all materials, including plastics, are important and crucial but, with 7.5B people already on this planet and with world population projected to increase to 11B people by 2050, and with our current waste disposal and resource issues having resulted from "disincentivizing" the people on this planet to engage in a "circular economy," I believe that, in addition to innovative product and waste disposal technology developments, we must also develop and implement incentives to motivate or force people to engage in making a circular economy happen.

Without offering a comprehensive review of the global plastics waste disposal issue, I will summarize my proposed guidelines for creating a viable future circular plastics economy.

1) Start with national deposit legislation which will increase the plastic PET bottle recycling rate from 15-20% to 70-80% and the number of pounds recycled from 3B to 5B, almost overnight! Today, 80+% of containers are returned in the (only) 10 deposit states while (only) 15-20% are returned in the 40 non-deposit states.

2) Follow that with a voluntary bottle/bag/ other return system that is sponsored by the plastics industry, and which would handle all packaging plastics. Check out the comprehensive voluntary return system that is already happening in Ann Arbor, MI at: https://www.recycleannarbor.org/services-guide/plastic-pollution-solution)

3) Follow that with state-sponsored programs to build (some) roads and (some) building materials out of mixed recycled plastics, as they have done in Australia and the Netherlands. Road and walkway paving (as a replacement for asphalt) and building blocks (as a replacement for cement) appear to be feasible solutions to using the mixed plastics waste stream, after we remove and recycle the high value PET and PE. In fact, there is a case for adding in crushed glass and other waste materials, using the mixed thermoplastics as a matrix and, using not-easily-recyclable plastics would solve the film and multilayer plastics issue. Early results suggest that mixed and not-easily-recyclable plastics could be used as high volume, durable, economical, and functionally appropriate, bulk paving and building materials and, if you search the Internet, you will find pilot projects that are well-along in Australia and the Netherlands. See, for example:

https://www.byfusion.com/byblock/ recycled-plastic/

https://www.betterworldsolutions.eu/portfolio/road-

4) Create a returnable plastics lottery system where reverse vending machines are used as slot machines and where any (authorized) plastic item could be deposited and where only very occasionally would the depositor win a (relatively) large dollar amount prize. The lottery mentality has been proven over many years to work effectively. That is, virtually everyone will consider buying a lottery ticket, knowing that the chance to win is 300 million to 1 but, also knowing that there is a (small) chance to win big. I guarantee you that a lottery system will bring back whatever plastic items we want to collect, just as deposit systems guarantee a high return rate for bottles. With a lottery system, we could include all types of plastic items ..... bottles, straws, cups, lids, plastic bags, whatever! Reverse vending machines that can identify and grind various plastics are already commercially available and every state has a lottery commission. Why not try it?

5) Finally, do everything possible to promote new technologies for recycling and to make recycling a profitable business opportunity.